© Crown copyright

First published 1995

Applications for reproduction should be made to HMSO

British Library Cataloguing in Publication Data

A catalogue record for this book is available from the British Library

ISBN 0 11 495745 2

FATHER FIGURES
Fathers in the Families of the 1990s

Edited by Peter Moss

Children

IN SCOTLAND

CLANN AN ALBA

working for children and their families

EDINBURGH: HMSO

CONTENTS

FOREWORD

Joanna Foster

The General Assembly of the United Nations showed great foresight when they chose 1994 as the International Year of the Family and set its theme as *Families: roles and responsibilities in a changing world*. So did Children in Scotland when they organised their International Year of the Family conference in Glasgow on the theme *Father figures, Fathers in the families of the 1990s*.

At this conference, the voices, views and visions of fathers confirmed what I learned in my travels in this country and overseas during 1994. Fathers feel strongly about their role in the family and they feel confused about the messages society is sending them about this role – messages which tell fathers how crucial their role is and how more active parenting and sharing of caring and family responsibilities is called for; these messages, however, are still contradicted by reality. It is not easy to be caring and sharing, still less to be caring and sharing and breadwinning.

The Glasgow conference about fatherhood reminded us that more than mere messages and exhortation were needed. A change in attitudes, in culture, and in policy and practice are also needed. To underline the point, the conference took place on the day the United Kingdom Government blocked a proposal for an EU Directive which would have given fathers, as well as mothers, the right to take leave to care for young children. All hope of an entitlement to even a single day's Paternity or Parental Leave disappeared on that day.

However, it was heartening to hear during 1994 more discussion and calls for family–friendly employment and to learn that enlightened organisations are realising that as the roles of men, as well as women, are changing the need for the reconciliation of work and family becomes a crucial issue for fathers as well as mothers. This need for more family-friendly employment is being increasingly recognised and is underscored by the recommendations made by the All-Party Parenting Group following four days of evidence during the International Year of the Family as well as by the recent findings of the House of Commons Employment Committee in their report on *Mothers in Employment.*

Now, in the campaign for better communication which I lead at the BT Forum, the priority issues are the changing roles of women and men as well as the balance between home and work. The position of men as fathers and, more broadly, as carers will be of particular importance in the debate we are seeking to stimulate and support.

CONTRIBUTORS

Søren Carlsen is the Specialist Consultant at the Secretariat of the Danish Equal Status Council and is the Leader of Nordic Council of Ministers' project on men's use of paternal leave entitlements. He works primarily on the Danish Government's Action Plan on equality and the relationship between working life and family life in an equality perspective.

Joanna Foster was the chair of the Council of the UK's Campaign of the UN's International Year of the Family 1994. She has chaired the Equal Opportunities Commission since 1988 and is now the Director of the BT Forum.

Sean French is a novelist and biographer, and he writes a weekly column in *New Statesman and Society*. His professional qualifications for the subject of this conference are that he edited the book, *Fatherhood*, which was published in 1992. His personal qualification is that he is the father of two children and stepfather to a further two.

Deborah Jones is a research assistant at the Department of Sociology, University of East London. She is currently completing her PhD on generational experiences of family and work for East London women.

Charlie Lewis is a lecturer in the Department of Psychology at the University of Lancaster. He has contributed to major texts on fatherhood, including *Becoming a Father* and *Reassessing Fatherhood*. His recent work has been on the subjects of how teenagers react to becoming fathers, fathers of children with behavioural difficulties and the effect of unemployment upon men.

Trefor Lloyd has been developing work with men for some 15 years. This has involved working with young men around issues of masculinity and sexism. He carried out an analysis of the media's view of father's and fatherhood for the European Commission Network on Childcare in 1994.

Peter Moss is a Senior Research Officer at the Thomas Coram Research Unit, at the Institute of Education, University of London, and is the Co-ordinator of the European Commission on Childcare. His publications include *Men as Carers*.

Margaret O'Brien is a Principal Lecturer in the Department of Sociology at the University of East London. She has been researching fatherhood for over a decade, beginning with her PhD on the experiences of lone fathers in the early 1980s. Her publications include the edited books *The Father Figure* and *Reassessing Fatherhood*.

Angela Phillips is a journalist and lecturer at Goldsmiths College, London. She is the author of *The Trouble with Boys* and has written about gender issues, the family and work for many years – indeed long before it became a fashionable issue!

Julie Smith has just completed her PhD in Child Health Epidemeology at the Institute of Child Health at Bristol University. Her thesis is based on tracing influences and trends in all aspects of infant care since 1950.

INTRODUCTION

Peter Moss

What future for fatherhood?

In September 1994, a conference was held in Glasgow – *Father Figures: fathers in the families of the 1990s*. The conference was organised by Children in Scotland and was a major event in the UK programme for the International Year of the Family. The conference offered a wide range of perspectives on fatherhood. This book brings together some of those perspectives, presenting contributions from most of the main speakers. In so doing, it offers only some of the ingredients that made up a rich and varied day. It does not include, for instance, the contributions from the floor or the conclusions from the wide range of workshops which covered such diverse issues as fathering after separation or divorce, men and physical punishment, men in child care, teenage fatherhood, issues in employment and fatherhood of children with special needs.

As Charlie Lewis says, in his concluding chapter, we are in a period of reassessment for fatherhood. There is a general awareness that fatherhood is not what it was. Fathers are losing their traditional roles – as authority figure, disciplinarian, the bridge between the family and the outside world, the breadwinner. In increasing numbers, they are also literally losing their place in the family, living apart from their children. This changed state of fatherhood is the product of a wider and complex process of demographic, economic, social and cultural change sweeping through European societies. These changes are contributing to a recasting of values, not least a decline in deference and respect for institutions and a new emphasis on individualisation.

While what fatherhood was is perhaps fairly clear, what it might become is less so. Some may seek a return to the old model. But this seems improbable; as Sean French comments, that model of fatherhood "was a part of a social and economic structure that is vanishing". Change cannot be wished away, especially when it is the product of such strong demographic, economic, social and cultural trends. Others see the father's role becoming increasingly marginal, possibly even redundant.

More hopefully, and emerging from debates in America and Europe in the 1980s, another view envisages an important, challenging but rewarding role, with a father, in the words of Angela Phillips, "who is loving, engaged, supportive and available, not only to his children, but also to his partner". The key requirements of fatherhood are being close, caring and emotionally involved, as well as actually sharing both the work and responsibility arising from the care and upbringing of children. Taking this view, the important question is not **whether** fathers are present in the family – for the painful reality is that in some cases children are likely to be better off not living with a father – but **how** they are present in the family.

Fatherhood of this kind offers opportunities to men, but also potentially to children. Angela Phillips argues that children have a right to a continuing emotional connection with both parents, even if those parents are not living together. She also draws attention to the potential damage that can be done to children, especially boys, by not having a close relationship with their father.

At the same time, attaining this participative and emotionally involved fatherhood is likely to prove both complex and difficult. Charlie Lewis reminds us that sex roles are produced by the interaction of several factors. Training and socialisation are critical. But how are boys and young men to achieve the training and socialisation necessary to sustain new relationships with children and partners? In fact, the experiences of many are more likely to militate against, rather than support, change. Angela Phillips argues that "an increasing number of young men are growing up in homes where their fathers have left or been pushed out and in which men are discussed in the most negative terms".

Even where fathers are present, they may not offer a positive role model. Violent fathers are an extreme but too common example. Less extreme but also problematic are the fathers who devote so much time to employment that they "exist for their children somewhere beyond the margins of day to day experience, who belong to them but are not available".

Positive role models outside the home are also few and far between. There is little positive public discussion about fathers and fatherhood. Having monitored much of the national press for a four week period in 1994, Trefor Lloyd draws a depressing conclusion: "there is a very limited debate within the media about fathers...little comment about what fathers are supposed to be, no guidance about how to be a father in the 1990s, with any pointers faltering after breadwinner and the general call on men to 'take more responsibility'".

Relations between family members also play an important part in shaping behaviour and ideas. Several contributors point out that women themselves are often confused and ambivalent about sex roles, both their own and their partners', being uncertain about whether they want to share the care of their children or keep it to themselves. Indeed, while the conference and this book necessarily pay attention to fathers, the role of fathers in families in the 1990s – or any other decade – cannot be considered in isolation from the role of mothers in those same families and the broader issue of gender relationships. The apparent ease with which women appear to have made the transition into the labour force, and their ability to cope with managing employment and family life, should not lead us to assume that the future of motherhood is any clearer or more easily arrived at than the future of fatherhood: as Charlie Lewis points out "recent analyses of motherhood suggest that women too find their experiences as challenging and confusing as men do theirs".

Finally, sex roles are determined by external relations between the family and the outside world. Of particular relevance here is the world of employment. The last ten years has seen a large increase in employment among mothers, especially those with young children; during the 1980s, the dual earner family became predominant in Britain, overtaking the one earner, two parent family (Brannen et al., 1994; Harrop and Moss, 1994). At the same time, other aspects of parental employment have shown little change. British fathers work the longest hours in Europe, averaging 47 hours a week in 1993; British mothers, at 24 hours a week, work the second shortest[1]. These long average hours of work mean many fathers spending large parts of their time at work, as well as travelling to and fro, at the expense of availability to children and partners and participation in family life.

The main way of managing the relationship between employment and family life in Britain's increasing number of dual earner families remains for the mother to take a part-time job, often involving very short hours worked at weekends or evenings (Brannen et al., 1994).

This pattern of male employment raises many problems, not only for fathers and children, but also for mothers, who lack support in the home and face a still dominant male pattern of employment that takes little notice of family responsibilities. At the same time, changes are occurring in employment which may increase, rather than decrease, barriers to change in fatherhood. Due to powerful, interrelated forces – the hegemony of free market ideology, increasing global competition, employers seeking maximum 'flexibility' in their use of labour, deregulation of labour markets, the weakening of organised labour, new technologies and production processes – the population of working age is increasingly segmented into three groups: the disadvantaged, who are out of work altogether; the marginalised, who have jobs that are insecure, poorly protected and carry few benefits; and the privileged, with relatively secure jobs. Will Hutton (1994) argues that this process is having a generally harmful effect on family life: "the fact that more than half the people in Britain who are eligible to work are living on poverty incomes or in conditions of permanent stress and insecurity... [means] it has become harder and harder for men and women in these circumstances to hold their marriages together, let alone parent their children adequately, as the hours of work in which a decent wage can be

---

[1] Both figures, which are for hours 'usually' worked, come from an analysis of the Labour Force Survey conducted by Eurostat for the EC Network on Childcare and Other Measures to Reconcile Employment and Family Responsibilities.

earned grow longer and longer" (p.109). More specifically, involuntary unemployment, insecure and unpredictable employment and the intensification of paid work do not provide an environment which encourages and enables men to respond to the changing employment position of women with children and to address the need for change in fatherhood.

Having recognised the difficulty and complexity of change, it is also important to recognise that changes have been happening – and not just negative changes. In Britain, some fathers are more involved with their children, are more participatory; since the end of the Second World War, as Julie Smith illustrates, there has been increasing involvement by fathers in the practical care of children, matched by changing attitudes to the role of fathers. Drawing on Nordic experience, Søren Carlsen concludes that "a process is underway in which the priority men give to the care of children is increasing – both in terms of what they want and their willingness to act"; in Sweden around half of all fathers now take some period of Parental Leave.

Change, however, is not uniform. As Margaret O'Brien and Deborah Jones note, different models of fatherhood and fathering are being negotiated in the home and we can see diverse forms of fathering taking place. There are divergent trends, with close and distant fatherhood models – being close, caring and emotionally committed on the one hand, and being marginal or altogether absent on the other – developing alongside each other.

This differentiation contributes to the difficulty of getting a clear view of what is actually happening. Broad brush surveys may not always be able to do justice to what is going on and answer questions about what types of change are occurring, for which fathers and in what families and starting from what baseline. The problem too is that change is often slow, and that what may be a steady but encouraging development to one person is slow and discouraging snail's pace change to another.

Fatherhood and public policy

Much of the change that has and will occur will be worked through within families and informal social networks – relatives and friends, local communities, workplaces. Sometimes change will result from explicit conflict, negotiation and agreement but more often perhaps it comes about through less overt and highly complex processes. Is there a role here also for public policy? Or is this, as some would insist, strictly private territory in which public policy has no role and is more likely to cause harm than provide help?

Government is already involved. The history of the Child Support Agency is a very clear example of a major policy intervention to reinforce a particular view of the role of fathers. Moreover, the absence of public intervention can be as much an expression of policy, and therefore a view of how things should be, as active intervention: for example, not to give men the right to Paternity Leave while giving women a right to Maternity Leave is a statement of values and beliefs about fatherhood and motherhood. Just as the general question is not "should there be change in the roles and relationships of fathers and mothers within the family?" but "what directions will change take?", so too the specific policy question is not "should there be a role for public policy?" but "how can public policy best be used to guide and support change?"

If, and it is a big if, the aim is to support the development of fatherhood that is loving, engaged, participative and available, paying far more attention to men's emotional and caring capacities in relation to children, then we are at the starting gates in this country as far as policy goes. The policy process has not begun to address this idea. Indeed, influential policy-makers may well find this particularly challenging because, since most are men who have a very high investment in paid work, the issues raised may be both distant from their daily concerns yet threatening if explored.

Two events occurring at the same time as the conference illustrate the point. The Employment Committee of the House of Commons was in the course of undertaking an enquiry into "mothers in employment". The enquiry, and its report published early in 1995 (House of Commons Employment Committee, 1995), beg important questions. While recognising that the needs of employed mothers deserve attention, why focus an enquiry on mothers? Why not enquire into "mothers

and fathers in employment" – unless it is implicitly assumed that fathers should not be equally responsible for children and unless it is taken for granted that fathers' employment is unproblematic and unrelated to mothers' employment? Why not consider the causes and consequences of the long hours many fathers spend at work? Why not examine how employment and caring for children can be reconciled for women **and** men?

Even more topically, the very week of the conference coincided with the UK Government again opposing, in the Council of Ministers of the European Union, a proposed Directive on Parental Leave, which would have given men as well as women the right to take time off work to care for a young child. In fact the proposed EU measure was very modest and unlikely to have led to many fathers taking this kind of leave. But it would have been a starting point, as well as a recognition of the importance of the father–child relationship.

There were two further striking features about this event. Media coverage was considerable, much more so than on previous occasions when the UK Government has blocked this proposal (which was first put forward by the European Commission in 1983). It was however poorly informed. The regular confusion of Parental Leave with Paternity Leave[1] in the press was symptomatic of a deeper ignorance about the issues involved. This was matched by the Government's response, an out of hand rejection of the proposed Directive without any public discussion of Parental Leave in general or of the EU proposal in particular, and without any actual evidence presented about the likely impact of such a measure on children, parents and employers.

Both events were missed opportunities. Britain urgently needs a sustained, informed and broad public discussion about

---

[1] Paternity Leave is a period of leave, only for fathers, to be taken at or near the time of childbirth. Parental Leave is a period of leave equally available to mothers and fathers, to enable either parent to provide care for their child. It is generally available after Maternity Leave finishes and is usually taken while children are under 3 years of age; however there is no intrinsic reason why Parental Leave cannot be available to be taken over a longer period of childhood.

policy measures such as Parental Leave, in the context of a wider debate about future directions for fatherhood and motherhood and the role of public policy in this evolutionary process. If, as Sean French concludes in his chapter, the father is no longer the symbol of authority that links the private world of the family with the public political realm, "what he can be is the sort of thing that honest politicians and policy makers ought to be discussing".

The Council of Ministers Recommendation on Child Care

In fact, the UK Government has made a commitment to take action to support change. But it has taken no steps to discuss either the commitment itself or how it might be implemented, another missed opportunity. In many ways, this commitment is the best kept secret in public policy!

In 1992, the UK Government, together with all other Member State Governments of the European Union, adopted a Council Recommendation on Child Care[1], and by so doing made a political commitment to the principles and objectives of the Recommendation. The Recommendation covers a range of measures needed to help men and women better reconcile employment with family responsibilities. Article 6 is particularly important to the subject of the conference and this book:

> As regards responsibilities arising from the care and upbringing of children, it is recommended that Member States should promote and encourage, with due respect for freedom of the individual, increased participation by men, in order to achieve a more equal sharing of parental responsibilities between men and women and to enable women to have a more effective role in the labour market.

So far, to the best of my knowledge, nothing has been done in the UK to implement Article 6 nor has it even been discussed. However, this year (1995) the UK Government must report to the European Commission about the measures it has taken to give effect to this Article and the rest of the Recommendation.

---

[1] 92/24/EEC OJ L 123, 8.5.1992

The inclusion of this Article in the Recommendation on Child Care is one example of the EU's long-standing interest in and commitment to the idea of fathers taking more responsibility for the care of children, as one of the conditions for achieving reconciliation between employment and family responsibilities which, in turn, is considered an essential condition for achieving one of the Union's objectives – gender equality in the labour market. Back in 1983, when the Commission first proposed a Directive on Parental Leave, the accompanying explanatory memorandum stressed that "the sharing of family responsibilities between parents is an essential part...of strategies designed to increase equality in the labour market" (European Commission, 1983; para. 4). Most recently, the 1994 European Commission White Paper on Social Policy refers specifically to this issue. New ways of sharing family responsibilities will "relieve the burden on women and allow men to play a more fulfilling role". Positive policy action is "needed to help the process of change". The Commission commits itself to "looking at ways of addressing the issues of stereotype roles of sexes in society" (European Commission, 1994; p.43).

Promoting and encouraging increased participation

The European Commission Network on Childcare and Other Measures to Reconcile Employment and Family Responsibilities, established in 1986 by the Commission's Equal Opportunities Unit, has been exploring how to promote and encourage increased participation by men in the care of children, following the lead provided by Article 6 of the Council Recommendation. The Network has produced a detailed report on leave arrangements for men and women with children in the EU (and Norway), including Maternity, Paternity and Parental Leave (EC Childcare Network, 1994a); it has monitored newspaper coverage of fathers and fatherhood in seven Member States (the chapter by Trefor Lloyd gives a brief overview of results from UK newspapers) (Deven, 1995); it is preparing a report on men working in childcare services; and it is involved in an Anglo–Italian project concerned with increasing fathers' participation in childcare services and the potential role of these services as places for supporting change in gender roles and relationships.

In 1993, the Network held an international seminar in Ravenna, in collaboration with the Regional Government of Emilia-Romagna in Italy (the Regional Government supported the seminar as part of a larger project on fatherhood, which is its response to the Recommendation on Child Care). This seminar reviewed measures already taken in a number of countries to encourage more equal sharing of family responsibilities between men and women. The Network's report on that seminar (EC Childcare Network, 1994b) covers a number of policy initiatives that have already been taken, in areas such as Parental Leave, community education and public awareness programmes, the use of childcare services and workplace initiatives – although it would have to be said that there was little to report in terms of workplace initiatives.

Such policy initiatives are vital, and I am sure there are many possibilities for action. But by themselves they are insufficient; we must go further than simply compiling a shopping list of things to do. Policies and other initiatives must be part of a carefully considered strategy for supporting and encouraging change, based on clear objectives and a detailed analysis of where the strategy is starting from (the economic, social and political context; the assets available to support change; the obstacles to change). The components of such a strategy are discussed fully in the seminar report, and I want to conclude this introduction by outlining some of these components.

First, there is no question of using public policy to force people to change – although it may be used to give more bargaining power to those who want to negotiate a more participant role for fathers. The main use for public policy is to work with people who want to change or feel that change is something they want to explore. It is also necessary to recognise that the prospect of change often creates ambivalent or negative feelings; both men and women may feel uncertain, even threatened, by the possibility of doing things differently. Men and women need safe and secure opportunities to explore their feelings about new gender roles and relationships.

Second, a successful strategy to support change must be based on a recognition of diversity in society – not only gender difference but other important dimensions such as class and ethnicity – and ensuring that measures are responsive to this diversity.

Third, change needs to be worked for in many settings and at many levels. We need national entitlements to Paternity and Parental Leave – but also initiatives at the level of individual nurseries, schools or workplaces and in other services and settings where people live their everyday lives. So, while a strategy may involve new measures and initiatives, it will build on and work through what already exists including services already well used by parents, media, community groups and so on.

Following from this need for a wide-ranging approach, not only will an effective strategy to support change need to involve public and private services used by families, it will also need to involve local authorities and employers and trades unions. They need to be invited and encouraged to give positive backing to national policies (for example, by supporting men in taking leave entitlements). But they also need to develop their own complementary policies and actions for their local areas and for specific workplaces.

Fourth, it may be particularly effective to target efforts on "golden opportunities" in life when men and women are more open to examining issues of equality, sharing, role and identity. These "golden opportunities" include major transition points in people's lives; for example, becoming a parent or grandparent.

Fifth, an important element in any strategy for change is the provision of role models – examples of individuals, families, workplaces, services actively working on issues of men as carers and more equal sharing of family responsibilities. Once again, this acknowledges the contribution of small-scale and local actions, as well as large-scale and national initiatives.

Sixth, appropriate and effective incentives to encourage and support change need to be identified. Incentives may take the form of specific policy devices (for example, extra payments for men taking leave). Alternatively, they may take the form of enabling men to consider and weigh up the personal benefits they may derive from taking more responsibility for the care and upbringing of children.

Finally, any strategy needs to recognise that change takes a long time, a point emphasised by Søren Carlsen on the basis of Scandinavian experience. This long haul will require sustained support from government, employers, trades unions and other organisations. It also needs regular reviews, taking account of changing circumstances and needs and assessing the extent and nature of change.

Underpinning the development and review process, there needs to be research. Charlie Lewis points to two important needs: to theorise more deeply about the reasons why some fathers become physically or psychologically absent from the family while others take a very active role; and to understand better the take-up (or lack of it) and consequences of specific policy measures such as Parental Leave. To this I would add a third priority: to explore and understand the barriers to change, for example fathers' employment, including patterns of employment (and unemployment), the reasons for and consequences of the way so many fathers are involved in employment and how the major changes occurring in the world of paid work are impacting on fathers.

Through developing such a strategy, public policy can play a part in supporting and encouraging movement towards fatherhood that is more involved and participatory. To say this is quite compatible with recognising the limitations of public intervention in a process that owes most to the interplay of complex social and economic forces within the family and the workplace. Together with workplace policies from employers and trades unions, public policy can contribute to cultural change, for example bringing discussion about fatherhood and caring for children into public discourse. It can provide some support and some increase in opportunities for men and women who want change in their lives and relationships, or who are at least interested in exploring change. It can influence the power balance in negotiations, in the family, the workplace or other settings where change in gender roles and relationships are determined.

The price of inaction

There are, of course, many forces working against change in the way fathers participate in families and relate to partners and children. Change is a complex, unpredictable and uneven process. But to do nothing, or to seek to revert fatherhood to an outmoded form, does a disservice to children, mothers, families – and fathers themselves.

Inaction perpetuates the continuing divorce between power and care, between those who make decisions and those who bring up the next generation. Increasing numbers of children will be denied a full relationship with both parents. More mothers will have to do more juggling of employment and caring for home and children, unable to compete with men at work unless they command financial resources enough to contract out caring for home and children to a new servant class. Tensions in family life will grow as more women question why they have to do so much juggling, while their partners continue at best to "help out".

Last but not least, men themselves will miss out on a unique opportunity for personal development and fulfilment, with most continuing instead to invest too much of their time, lives and personalities in the increasingly fickle and precarious world of employment. This loss of opportunity is part of the price of inaction in public policy, as well as inaction by employers and trades unions. But it is also the price of inaction by men themselves. The questions that spring continually to mind in reading the chapters in this book are not only "what can be done to encourage and support change in men's relationships with their children and in their involvement with their children's care and upbringing?", but also "how much do men want and recognise the need for change?" and "what are men prepared to do to get change?"

References

Brannen, J., Mészáros, G., Moss, P. and Poland, G. (1994) *Employment and Family Life: a review of research in the UK (1980-1994)*, (Research Series No. 41), Sheffield: Employment Department

Deven, F. (1995) *Men, Media and Child Care*, Brussels: European Commission Equal Opportunity Unit

European Commission (1983) *Proposal for a Council directive on Parental Leave and Leave for Family Reasons: Explanatory Memorandum* (COM (83) 686, 22 November 1983

European Commission (1994) *European Social Policy, a Way Forward for the Union*, Luxembourg: Office for Official Publications of the European Communities

EC Childcare Network (1994a) *Leave Arrangements for Workers with Children*, Brussels: European Commission Equal Opportunity Unit

EC Childcare Network (1994b) *Men as Carers: towards a culture of responsibility, sharing and reciprocity between women and men in the care and upbringing of children*, Brussels: European Commission Equal Opportunity Unit

Harrop, A., and Moss, P. (1994) 'Working parents: trends in the 1980s', *Employment Gazette*, 102 (10), 343-352

House of Commons Employment Committee (1995) *Mothers in Employment (Volume 1: Report and Proceedings of the Committee)*, London: HMSO

Hutton, W. (1994) *The State we're in*, London: Jonathan Cape

FATHER FIGURES

Chapter 1

THE FALLEN IDOL

Sean French

A couple of months ago my wife was away on business for a couple of days and I looked after the children on my own. When my three-year-old daughter was describing this experience to her grandmother – my mother – she told her that she had slept in my bed with me. My mother mentioned this to me and added in a half-joking sort of way that I had better look out or I might get into trouble.

I am not sure whether I should have been alarmed by this warning – or insulted. But my first reaction was that if my own mother could talk in this way, even humorously, it was a sign of social change. Another bit of fatherhood had been chipped away from us. Those of us trying to be fathers already knew that we could not be Victorian patriarchs and that we did not want to be; but maybe we could aspire to the condition of motherhood. Instead of being stern, distant, the dispenser of punishment, we would be benign, tactile, nurturing. The kinder, gentler father, to use George Bush's words. The father who was at ease with himself, to paraphrase John Major.

But now this has been tainted as well. In Sylvia Plath's poem, 'Daddy', the old-style father was described as a fascist. The new-style, hands-on father is liable to be reported to the social services and denounced as an abuser. Perhaps he is an abuser, whether he knows it or not. I have already read an opinion piece in the *Guardian* by a woman arguing that non-sexual contact between fathers and daughters, casual nudity and tactility, is a form of assault that is psychologically damaging. And we should stop it. How does she know that it is damaging? But then how do I know that it is not? We can debate the details of arguments like this, but the larger point is that fatherhood has become a major issue in British politics at the very moment when it has become, in any traditional terms, irretrievable. Because fatherhood has always been more than a biological relation, the authority of the father over his family has traditionally been a validating symbol of all the larger social forms of authority, of law, society and religion. And this authority in its very essence is a male.

Roger Scruton, the conservative thinker, put it eloquently in an essay on fatherhood, all the more so because he so deeply regrets the loss of patriarchal authority. In his words:

> *When God the Father destroys his creation he does not destroy himself, as a mother would, but only reaffirms himself as something higher. So God rebuked the world by flooding it. This does not mean that a Divine Father loves less than a Divine Mother; but he loves more severely. His love takes the form of law: 'thou shalt', and 'thou shalt not'. His children must earn his love through their obedience. His voice sounding within them has the tone of a command, while the voice of a mother is ever soft with new excuses.*
>
> *A mother is vulnerable in her children; a father is vulnerable to them. For he runs the risk of rebellion. To adopt his role is to become a judge, to assume the rightness of his own position, and a title to obedience. It is to close a door on all excuses, and to make justice and mercy his own. The father's position, therefore, is supremely lonely. Of course, the priest who is father to his flock can rest his case in a higher power. Father upon father stand in rank behind him, on the ladder of authority that reaches up to God. But in a godless world fathers suffer a dreadful loss of confidence. What if the only ground of my command is that I command it? Can I still cast my love as an edict, and expect my children to shape themselves through their obedience?*

We feel ambivalent about the very word "father" now, just as we do about the language of control; words like authority, law, punishment. In our post-enlightenment language, the notion of authority has been replaced by the notion of oppression. In the same way our image of the stern but just patriarch, so glowingly recalled by Scruton, has been replaced by the image of the bully, venting his own frustrations on his partner and children

We ought to be ambivalent about the idea of fatherhood and I am alarmed by the people who are not, who see it as simply one of the options for crime reduction. When politicians call for the return of the responsible father, of the importance of the father figure within the nuclear family, they are also calling for a return of the whole system of authority. They do it in the same disingenuous spirit in which they lament the decline in churchgoing and call for the clerics to take a moral lead. It may be that the crime rate would fall if more people believed in God and went to church – though even that is debatable – but you can't legislate for belief in God as a way of reducing crime.

Politicians who talk of the importance of the father as the figure of authority in the family, as the role model for growing boys, ignore their own role in undermining that very authority. Fatherhood was a part of a social and economic structure that is vanishing. The father's relation to the house over which he presided was defined, for example, by the fact the he left it every day, that he worked in order to provide for it, that he returned in the evening with his rewards and punishments. In the modern economy of long-term unemployment, casualisation, short-term contracts, female part-time work, it has become increasingly difficult for fathers to do the sort of things that fathers are meant to do.

Of course, one of the multiple ironies of the whole discussion is that while absent fathers are a problem in many poor families, there are many families where fathers are more present than ever before. It is no accident that this year has seen the first admission of the word "cocooning" into Chambers' Dictionary, in its new sense of spending your time largely with your immediate family rather than with a wider social network.

It could be argued that motherhood is less vulnerable to social change; however, women's lives may alter under social and economic pressures. Women still become pregnant, give birth and it seems, increasingly breastfeed. However feckless a mother is, however disadvantaged, however discontented with her state, she will still be present at the birth.

After the moment of conception, fatherhood has always been more of an idea, a social construct, and now it looks like a myth as well. What is it to be a father? We are all abnormal now, and I can cite my own situation as typically atypical. My wife has two children from a previous marriage and we have had two further children. I have two brothers, my wife's previous husband has a brother. So there is a plethora of father figures, and grandfather figures and uncle figures. Tony Blair and Professor A. H. Halsey would be proud of us. Unfortunately there is only one boy to benefit from all of this. The three girls have to make do with just one mother figure between them.

We are also conventionally unconventional in our economic arrangements. I work at home, in irregular freelance employment, while my wife goes out to work in an office. I am always hanging around making cups of tea, she comes through the door at about six-thirty. Yet social novelty, even of this mild kind, poses problems for everybody. The daughter I mentioned earlier obsessively plays a game with her friend in which one is the mother and the other is the baby. I have repeatedly asked her where the father is and she always replies that the father has gone out to work. For her, a father who goes out to work is as real as a unicorn, but such are the pressures of the culture to which she is exposed.

The reason I took a particular interest in the meaning of modern fatherhood was because it was a question I had to negotiate in my own life. What sort of figure was I to the two children to whom I am related? And what sort of figure am I to the two children who have a father of their own, but who spend most of their time with me? Any straightforward answer to those questions is likely to be wrong. And in the past couple of years I have also been interested to discover that it is families like mine – if I can use so patriarchally possessive a term as "mine" – that are to blame for what's wrong with Britain.

I remember that at the end of 1993, Professor A. H. Halsey, the sociologist and self-styled ethical socialist, jumped on the family bandwagon from a leftward direction: "Socialism," he said, "is traditional family values extended to the wider community." He considered that feminism had been a "mixed bag". The adults had gained at the expense of the children. It was not clear whether this insight had derived from his "sound scientific analysis" or his "common sense", both of which he referred to, but it was clear that he had constructed an idealised version of the family to function like one of those cure-alls that were sold by travelling salesmen at American fairs: "The Old-Fashioned Family", guaranteed to stop ram-raiding, reverse the economic decline of Britain, halt teenage pregnancy, stop those feckless feminists, and get dinner on the table when the ethical socialist gets home from a hard day of sound scientific analysis at his office.

I think it is astonishing to find a sociologist blaming feminism for the changes that have taken place in family life. Is it responsible, for example, for the shift in male and female employment patterns in Wales over the last ten years? And we talk of spreading family values through society. It sounds like such an unanswerably good thing, but if families mean nurturing and mutual respect, they can also mean nannying, interference, bitter conflict. There are plenty of countries in the world that are like families, where it is like a Christmas Day get-together every day of the year with all the squabbles, sulks, rows and depressions as well as the exhilaration that goes with that. The Bosnian catastrophe is like a family quarrel with mortars and rockets. South Africa was on the brink of civil war because of the elevation of tribal, family values over individual rights.

There is nothing intrinsically good about family values or about the father as one of the embodiments of these values. A good father is a good thing, a bad father is a bad thing. This might seem tiresomely self-evident, except that right wing think tanks have been talking about the father the way that Woody Allen once talked about sex. A good father is good, a bad father is still pretty good. He simply needs to be there, like a totem pole, and all sorts of laws and punitive financial sanctions are being considered to keep him there.

Social historians would doubtless argue about whether the confident, authoritative, reassuring father ever existed. Whether he did or not, he will not be legislated back into existence just because we are worried about ram-raiding and truancy. There will still be fathers, of course, of many different kinds, and I hope that as many as possible will stay around to bring up the children and help with the washing-up while they are there. But as the central symbol of authority that links the private world of the family with the public political realm, the father is in as many pieces as Humpty Dumpty. That is not what the father is. What he can be is the sort of thing that honest politicians and policy makers ought to be discussing.

THE TROUBLE WITH BOYS

Chapter 2

THE TROUBLE WITH BOYS

Angela Phillips

Over the last year I have been approached on a number of occasions by television programmes wanting me to pronounce, in about three minutes, for, or against, fathers. They come up with soundbite titles such as "are fathers really necessary?" On each occasion I have had to explain that I do not think fathers are something one can simply take sides on. It is like asking me whether I am in favour of trees because fathers, like trees, exist already. It is far too late to ask whether we need them! And like trees, they can be beautiful, provide shade, be a place to climb and play or they may need to be uprooted because they are undermining the foundations of your house.

The vast majority of children do have fathers, even if they see them rarely or not at all. So the question is not really whether fathers are necessary but whether fathers and mothers must live together in order to create children who are, emotionally at least, properly formed. Even here the answer is far from simple.

Right wing American economist Charles Murray talks about the family as though fathers were cogs in the wheels of a machine and the lack of a father will create a child with a specific component missing. Stick the cog back in and then all will come right. More than that, he seems to think that women are wilfully sabotaging the machine – to the detriment of the rest of society.

There is no doubt that fathers can be extremely influential but that influence is not necessarily benign. The worst father a boy can have is not one who is missing but one who teaches him to be bad. We know, for example, that the boys most likely to offend are not those without fathers but those whose fathers are themselves criminals. In other words, where there is a father in the house, and that father is a lousy father, then the son is more likely to get into trouble than if he was not there at all. Similarly, a man who beats his wife is teaching his son that women can be beaten, and a man who beats his son may well turn him into someone who sees violence as the only way to get what he wants. He may learn these lessons from other men too but a father does, without doubt, have a greater influence than other men. Losing a father like this would not be a great loss to a child.

On the other hand, a father who is loving, engaged, supportive and available, not only to his children, but also to his partner, is clearly a bonus, because having two loving people in his life will make a child feel safer and because children learn from the way their parents behave towards each other as well as the way they are themselves treated and also, for a boy, because seeing an adult man who is loved and loving provides him with a sense that he too can grow up to be like that.

Given the complexity of family relationships, any suggestion that there should be pressure forcing parents to stay together "for the sake of the children" is simplistic and, by definition, misguided. Clearly some children are far better off living with lone mothers than putting up with the fathers that fate has dealt to them. Similarly there will be children with ineffectual mothers whose best hope of growing to full and positive adulthood would be to leave her well behind.

Nevertheless, the separation between fathers and children does create a problem, particularly for boys, because the absence of men in their lives leaves them with a gap in their sense of what a man should be. Girls have their mothers to look to for a sense of how to be a good adult. Boys whose fathers are inadequate, angry, or just absent, often learn to see adult masculinity through the distorting mirror of their mothers' fear, disappointment, or disgust. They see adult men as people who are deficient and they imagine that they will grow up to be deficient in the same way. Just as women turned the weakness of their dependency around and called it their natural role, so these young men will see that men are regarded as emotionally withdrawn or aggressive and call that their natural masculinity.

The problem with fathering today is far bigger than the matter of the high divorce rate. It is about men whose names are on the mortgage or the rent book but who barely ever come through the door during their children's waking hours. Why do so many men feel the need to work eleven hours a day and then start again at the weekend? After all, even in families where both parents work, the father will almost always work longer than the mother. Is it really the demands of the boss or the demands of peer group pressure, the workday equivalent of being the biggest goal scorer in the playground? Why do policy makers moan about the influence of absent fathers among the unemployed without recognising that employment is an even bigger cause of father absence in families with jobs?

It is these ordinary everyday "muddle though" kind of fathers that interest me. The kind who do care about their kids but are not quite sure how to show it. The men who exist for their children somewhere beyond the margins of day-to-day existence, who belong to them but are not available to them. I spoke to an eight-year-old boy living in a two parent family, about what he does with his father after school, and he said: "I don't talk to him much because he is always working. But I watch him."

In the past, father absence of this kind has been tolerated. After all, mothers were always there to provide the anchor of their children's lives and everything we have learned about children in this post-Freudian world tells us that children need most of all to feel valued, and through being valued learn how to value themselves. A father could simply move in and out of the family home providing a distanced role model. One which appeared to suffice for his sons because it taught them just how to be as distanced as he was. You know the sort: tweed suit, briar pipe, leaning on the car at the door of a suburban semi.

In fact, as I go into in much greater detail in my book, *The Trouble with Boys* (Phillips, 1993), it is a distance which creates a vacuum and in that vacuum boy children construct an idea of themselves built partly on the father they can see out of the corner of the eye but more surely on the behaviour of their peers. It is in the playground, not at home, that a boy learns to be a man. As one young man put it to me, quite seriously:

"Football taught me the basic rules of interpersonal relationships."

In the old world this cardboard cut-out view of self seemed to work reasonably well. Boys learned to read, write, fight and make alliances in school and then went out to do the same things in the world of work. They were not called upon to be emotional or nurturing so they were unlikely to discover their deficiencies in this respect.

But now everything else in the world has changed. Mothers still provide the major emotional prop in most homes but they are no longer prepared to be the doormat as well. They want from their partners what, in the past, they would have got from mothers, sisters and friends: someone to give practical and emotional support in the home so that they too can go out into the world. (I do not for a minute suggest that women are all sorted and men are all confused about this. I am well aware that many women are just as uncertain about whether they want to share the care of their children or keep it to themselves, but now we are discussing fathers.) But men are not trained for the role women are coming to expect from them and too often their own conditioning means they do not even know how to ask. As a result an awful lot of men and women are very angry with each other for failing to be the person they expected them to be.

Into this changing world children have been born willy-nilly. Not many people stop breeding in order to get their lives sorted out. They just live in hope. Yet children need certainty. Or at least a degree of stability. And they want to know that the people they are going to become are good people, people who are worth becoming. We know what a difference it has made to girls to grow up knowing that girls can be everything and do everything. Girls are doing better than ever at school, and feel far more able than ever before to live independent lives. Girls know that they do not need men even if they may want them. That they can have a job, and a baby, even if Mr Right does not come along or only drops by on a temporary basis.

What are we telling our boys? They are learning that a man's role in the world is conditional. That they will be tolerated only if they can earn enough money. As young men they are classed as yobs and have become the focus of a government hate campaign every bit as unpleasant as last year's campaign against their mothers. As fathers they are noticed in government policy only when they have left their families and even then only in terms of the maintenance they can pay. During the week of the conference, the government vetoed a proposed EU Directive on Parental Leave and proposed £1000 fines on parents of persistent offenders – strange priorities. A man is only considered worthwhile if he is a football player, a president, head of a corporation, or a major criminal. For a boy, the gulf between himself and the possibility of being a good man, a successful man, a worthy and noticed man, is vast indeed.

One thing most boys will become one day is a father but they know even less about that than they do about football because they have had virtually no contact with a real person who fulfils this role. When a young woman becomes a mother for the first time she may think she is operating directly from a baby-care book but gradually her long repressed memories of being mothered will find their way into her fingertips, her voice, the way she moves and rocks her child. Many young men these days are having to invent the role of father as they go along. For some, the invention will be far more positive than the role they might have learned by watching and absorbing their own father's behaviour. Research among full-time 'primary nurturing fathers' for example has found that many of them were brought up in families without fathers and that their caring behaviour seems to have been modelled on mothering rather than fathering.

But there is no doubt that increasing numbers of young men are growing up in homes where their fathers have left or been pushed out and in which men are discussed in the most negative terms. These boys will have absorbed the idea that a man is a law unto himself, that caring for children is women's business and that, since women do not think much of adult men, they may as well get what they can in the short term and spend the rest of the time with the lads. What sort of fathers can these young men be to their own children? If they do not believe that men are loveable then they will not trouble to try to be loveable to their children.

The issue at stake here is nothing to do with the rights of adults, the independence of women, or even the economy. Nor is it to do with the preservation of the family. It is to do with the rights of children. A child who feels unloved by a parent, will feel pain, loss and grief and he feels a less important person because he failed to retain the love and support of that person. He may also feel anger – and burning resentment – at the mother who, in his eyes, deprived him of that connection. It is this feeling of loss and anger from which we must protect our children even if we, as adults, would like to walk away; because a child who feels less important, less loved, will take time to recover and may, in that time, lose sight of the fact that he is worth loving. These are the children who are at risk to themselves and a risk to the rest of us.

The vast majority of children are born to two parents (even when their parents are not married). They have a right to a continuing emotional connection with both parents whether or not their parents are together and it is this connection which provides the challenge for the future of fatherhood. Are men capable of rising to it and will women be prepared to move over and allow them in?

Many men have difficulty maintaining relationships with their children after a marriage has ended. Some have simply never got to know their children and have no idea of their own importance as parents; others, unable to cope with the emotional demands of the situation, simply withdraw (after all is not that what boys are trained to do from the earliest days). But in some cases it is the mother who forces the breakdown. I cannot find it in me to support a mother who deliberately moves to another part of the country, or to another country, in order to shake off the father of her children just because she wants to feel independent. I did not believe that women could behave like that once – now I know that they can. We have the right to get rid of a partner we do not want any more, but we do not have the right to deprive a child of his or her parent.

Families in which there are no adult men may teach daughters that women can be independent from men but they also make a statement to sons which says "your place is out there in the world, fending for yourself. Here in this family, is a place for women and children." Women need the possibility of lone parenthood because it is that possibility which has made us strong. It is only in the last twenty years that we have had the power to say to men who mistreat or abuse us, "get lost, I won't put up with you." But, while I would defend the rights of single mothers (after all I am one) the lone mother family is not a model I would hold up as either egalitarian or progressive. It is the model we came from: women together raising children and men free to create war, to control trade, to forge the lines on which society will be modelled.

There is not a simple solution. It will come slowly because it will take first of all something of a revolution amongst men. If women and men are to share the upbringing of their children they must first of all find a better way of relating to each other and that means moving towards a real understanding of gender equality. It sounds impossible but I have to believe that, deep down, it is what men want too. Women give birth to both boys and girls. They are equally connected to us. And I think those of us who are mothers want the best for all our children. I for one do not relish the thought of a world in which men are like rogue elephants, roaming the periphery of family life, allowed in only for mating.

References

Phillips, A. (1993) *The Trouble with Boys*, London: Pandora

Chapter 3

THE FIRST INTRUDER
Fatherhood, a historical perspective

Julie Smith

Introducing the project *Yesterday, Today...Tomorrow*

In this chapter, I will discuss changes that have occurred in attitudes to fatherhood and practical infant care tasks since 1950, and give some initial results from a population-based study conducted in the Avon area which show changes over time in levels of paternal involvement in these tasks.

The study, *Yesterday, Today...Tomorrow (YTT)*, is a sub-study of the Avon Longitudinal Study of Pregnancy and Childhood – popularly known as the *Children of the 90s* study. The *YTT* study covers a time period of four complete decades – 1950s, 60s, 70s, 80s – and 1990/91. The sample of mothers for the *YTT* study came from two sources. The 1990/91 mothers came from the large data-base for the *Children of the 90s* study; the rest of the sample was obtained through mothers in the *Children of the 90s* study enrolling other, older mothers of their acquaintance; this was easier than advertising and also led, we felt, to less possibility of bias (since mothers recruited through advertising would be more likely to be highly motivated). The numbers of mothers included in the study were 99 (1950s), 94 (1960s), 69 (1970s), 158 (1980s) and 286 (1990/91).

Information on ethnic group was not asked for, so it is not possible to say how representative the sample was on this parameter. However, social class was more or less equally distributed for each decade group. Throughout the study, 95–100% of fathers were living with the mothers of their children and assumed to be in stable relationships during the first year of their child's life.

Levels of paternal involvement during the first year of the child's life were assessed for the pre-1990s decades by asking several questions of the mothers: "did you get any help with the care of your infant?"; "who gave that help? (husband/partner, mother, relative, friend, nanny)"; "what part did your husband/partner take in the care of your infant? (bathing/feeding/walking/putting to bed)". Mothers from the 1990s sample were also asked if they got any help with the care of their infant, but were asked how often their husband/partner undertook specific tasks, such as bathing.

The results are clear. They show a definite increase throughout the study period in paternal involvement with the practical care of their babies. Just over a third (38%) of the 1950s mothers reported that they got help with the care of their infant from husbands or partners; among the 1990s mothers, the proportion was over three-quarters (82%) (Figure 1).

Figure 1
Paternal Involvement with practical infant care tasks

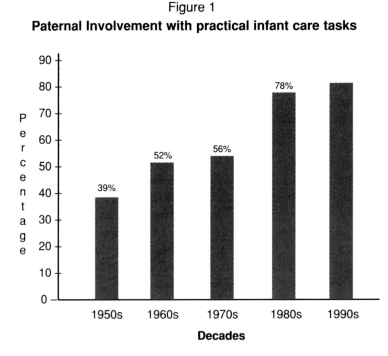

Decades

Changing attitudes to fatherhood

There appear to have been many assumptions made about the role of the father throughout the study period. Historical accounts tend to reveal a stereotype based on traditional views. Information about fathers has often been gathered from mothers. On a practical note, mothers are usually far more accessible to researchers than fathers are and there is no doubt that female dominance of child care is an accepted "norm" in our society.

Pre-1950 there is little or no mention by baby-care experts of a father's role within the province of infant care. Truby-King makes no mention of fathers at all and Bertrand Russell (1929) leaves us in little doubt of his opinion:

> *No doubt the ideal father is better than none but many fathers are so far from ideal that their non-existence might be a positive advantage to children.*

By the 1940s, though, it appears that some men were having their say about their role as fathers. I came across a transcript of a "Woman's Hour" programme in 1949 (January 4), where a new father was asking "Why leave Dad out of it?" He put forward the view that men should have practical involvement with their infants. The presenter, Joan Griffiths, concludes the programme with these words:

> *So all fathers should learn how to fix a baby comfortably in a nappy without sticking a pin in him and learn lots of other useful things like how to hold the baby the right way up.*

In the 1950s it was being acknowledged that fathers were taking on some of the care tasks for their infants. Phyllis Hostler (1953) describes the father as "the first intruder into the magic circle of mother and child". The Illingworths (1964) allow the father to be an "emergency carer" who is not expected to be as proficient as the mother but can just about muddle through. But the 1950s and 60s image of the father was one of clumsiness and exasperation, of kindly, patronising tolerance for their attempts to be useful. If we take the example of bathing a baby, the Newsons (1963) found that it was the task least likely to be undertaken by a father – the reason for this was the fear of dropping, hurting or even drowning the baby on both the mothers and the fathers part. By contrast, the *Children of the 90s* study shows that this is now the most popular of the infant care tasks that fathers perform; Figure 2 shows the increase throughout the study period of men bathing their infants.

Figure 2

Percentage of fathers bathing their infants

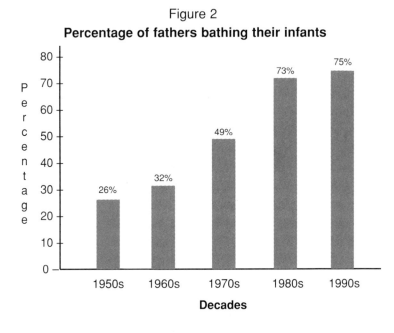

The role of the father was not one that was created by men, according to David Mace in an article "Baby Brings A Crisis" in *Woman* magazine (May 1951):

Nature does not implant in the father the same blind devotion to the baby as it does in the mother. Every man is not by instinct a parent. Fatherhood is something that he has to grow into – and sometimes he needs help... the wife must take upon herself the task of making her husband into a father.

By the 1960s, attention was being paid to the emotional aspects of becoming a father, as illustrated by this excerpt from a BBC radio programme "Parents and Children" (June 18, 1962):

In a strange way he may secretly envy [the mother] her creativity, although perhaps he would be the last to admit it. His part was so quick and unnoticed.

Although this can be seen as rather amusing, it does reveal the sense of inadequacy fathers were assumed to feel about the whole process of procreation; once the conception was achieved they had no further involvement. However, Dr John Gibbens, a leading child care expert in the 1940s through to the 1960s, did see a definite role for fathers. He advised new fathers to get an allotment, grow fresh vegetables, keep interfering relatives at bay and take out an insurance policy for the school fees!

In the 1970s and 80s, a new element in attitudes to fatherhood emerges. Academic studies start to take place asking fathers directly about their feelings and involvement with their infants. Leaflets appear at antenatal clinics directed at fathers, with titles like *It's Your Baby Too* and *Being Dad*. Just as "bonding" became fashionable in the 1970s for mothers so it was that fathers were to be encouraged to release their "inner caring mechanisms".

Influences on growing paternal involvement

Lorna McKee and Margaret O'Brien (1982) suggest in their work that paternal attendance at birth is one way in which subsequent paternal "bonding" could be affected. The *YTT* study gathered information on both paternal attendance at birth and subsequent paternal involvement in the practical aspects of infant care. Table 1 shows the percentage of fathers attending the birth of their first-born child throughout the study period. This reveals a large increase in the number of fathers who attended over the course of the study period.

Table 1. Paternal attendance at birth of first infant, 1950s – 1990s

Decade	Paternal attendance at birth
1950s	5% (5/99)
1960s	10% (9/94)
1970s	35% (24/69)
1980s	90% (142/158)
1990s	97% (270/286)

Whether this attendance serves to promote "bonding" of the father with his infant is difficult to assess. However results from the YTT study, using the Mantel Hientsel test for association over time, demonstrate a strong association over time between paternal presence at birth and subsequent involvement with practical infant care tasks (Table 2). This lends some support to the proposition that attendance at the birth does promote "bonding".

Table 2. The association over the study period of paternal attendance at birth of first born infants and subsequent involvement with practical infant care tasks

Decade	%%%	P value	Odds Ratio	95% C.I.
1950s	20% (1/5)	0.362	0.36	0.10:1.31
1960s	56% (5/9)	0.803	1.20	0.70:1.94
1970s	67% (16/24)	0.219	1.91	1.45:2.50
1980s	83% (118/142)	0.000		
1990s	56% (144/270)	0.900	0.91	0.22:3.74

Mantel Heintsel test, stratifying for decade of birth: relative risk estimate = 1.96 revealing a 95% Confidence Interval of 1.13:3.40.

However, from the 1990s data it is known that a quarter of the 97% of fathers who attended the birth of their first-born child did so under pressure. These fathers were selected and their subsequent involvement with practical infant care tasks was measured. Nearly two-thirds (61%) of the fathers who stated that they had felt pressured to be at the birth were subsequently reported as not involved in the practical care of their infants (Table 3). Although the difference is not statistically significant, the percentage of men who were stated not to have subsequent involvement with practical infant care tasks is somewhat higher among fathers who felt pressurised to attend their child's birth than among fathers who did not feel pressurised. Overall, it appears that although paternal attendance at birth does show an association with subsequent involvement, this may be influenced in turn by the attitude of the father to this attendance. A father who feels pressured to be there may not find the attendance helpful for his subsequent "bonding" with his infant.

Brian Jackson undertook research on the subject of fathers in the early 1980s. His study, based in Bristol, found that

Table 3. The association between fathers' feelings of being pressured to attend the birth of their first infant and subsequent involvement with practical infant care (early 1990s)

If felt pressured to attend	Subsequent Involvement	No Involvement
Yes	39% (26/67)	61% (41/67)
No	44% (90/203)	56% (114/203)

P value = 0.445; Odds Ratio = 0.803; 95% Confidence Interval = 0.46:1.41.

existing academic literature was largely limited to abnormal fathers – fathers who were absent from the home through divorce, imprisonment, death or mental illness. Little had been said about the normal, everyday Dad, who as far as the literature available was concerned seemed to be an invisible figure. Therefore he chose to study 100 first time fathers who had normal, healthy babies and were in stable relationships. He achieved a 100% response rate in his study, which he attributed to the novelty value of the study itself, although one of the first things he noticed was the confusion of mothers who wondered why anyone would want to talk to the fathers of their children. This he attributed to a "cultural incomprehension" (Jackson, 1984).

A national cohort study of children born in 1970 had found that 40% of men came home to a sleeping child and 11% of those men were not there at the weekend either; consequently time, irrespective of quality of contact, was severely limiting in the building of paternal relationships. But by the early 1980s, when Brian Jackson was conducting his study, rising unemployment had begun to change the traditional equation of man plus work equals mother and child. Large numbers of men were spending more time with their children even if it was forced through unemployment.

Brian Jackson asked "Did men actually want to spend more time with their children and less time at work?" He found that there was an overall increase in paternal involvement with infant care in comparison to previous studies. It could be argued that any increase in paternal involvement is associated with the increase in paternal unemployment and more women returning to employment outside of the home; in this case, increased paternal involvement could stem purely from financial necessity. Brian Jackson, however, felt that the change in paternal involvement that he observed had not occurred as a result of changes either in education or in employment and unemployment, but was due to a shift in the emotional needs of men to be closely involved with their offspring. In short, men were showing an increased desire to be involved.

Results from the *YTT* study support Brian Jackson's conclusion. Among the study sample, the proportion of mothers who had returned to work outside the home before their child's first birthday rose from 8% in the 1950s to 55% in the 1990s. Although more women have returned to work after childbirth, forcing a change in the division of labour within the home, infant care while mothers are at work has been mainly the province of female carers rather than fathers. In the early 1990s, only 26% of the study mothers who returned to employment stated that their husband/partner took care of their baby whilst they were at work; the main sources of care were childminders (28%), friends (30%) and a grandparent or other relative (44%)[1].

Table 4 shows the maternal employment rate for the study mothers in each decade and the frequency of paternal involvement in practical infant care tasks. Tests show no statistically significant relationship between these two variables, either for any one decade or over time (Table 5). The reasons for the increase in paternal involvement in infant care,

Table 4. Levels of maternal employment and paternal involvement in practical infant care over the study period

Decade	Maternal Employment	Paternal Involvement
1950s	8% (8/99)	39% (39/99)
1960s	16% (14/96)	52% (49/96)
1970s	16% (11/69)	56% (39/69)
1980s	47% (73/158)	78% (123/158)
1990s	55% (154/286)	82.5% (236/286)

Table 5. The association over the study period of maternal employment and paternal involvement in practical infant care

Decade	%%%	P value	Odds Ratio	95% C.I.
1950s	62.5% (5/8)	0.164	0.60	0.24:1.48
1960s	36% (5/14)	0.206	1.40	0.88:2.23
1970s	60% (6/11)	0.820	0.91	0.40:2.06
1980s	79.5% (58/73)	0.693	0.89	0.49:1.61
1990s	53% (64/146)	0.923	1.01	0.77:1.76

Mantel Heintsel test, stratifying for decade of birth reveals a relative risk estimate of 1.03 and a 95 % Confidence Interval of 0.70: 1.53.

[1]The percentages come to more than 100 because some mothers reported using more than one type of care.

therefore, need to be sought in factors other than parental employment patterns.

Conclusion

Paternal involvement in infant care can be seen to be central to the whole debate surrounding gender roles in society. The *YTT* study has revealed an increase in paternal involvement with practical infant care tasks and there also appears to be an increase in the acknowledgement of fathers as carers of infants.

A feminist explanation of the move towards greater paternal involvement in the home is that it is just another means by which men exert power over women. Not content, so this argument goes, with browbeating women in the market place, men have replicated this dominance in the field of child care – traditionally an area of female authority. Such an argument seems to be contradictory – women fought to be released from the restrictions that motherhood placed on them, such as the loss of continuity of employment or career prospects and yet seem to resent the increased involvement of fathers.

Brian Jackson's study of 100 first time fathers in Bristol in 1984 concludes that "to release the full force of fatherhood will mean breaking the masculine taboo on tenderness". Although there are a great many reasons for the increase in paternal involvement with the care of young children, perhaps there are indications that the "masculine taboo on tenderness" if not actually broken has at least been dented a little.

References

Gibbens, J. (1962) *Care of Young Babies*, London: Churchill

Hostler, P. (1953) *The Child's World*, London: Benn

Illingworth, R. and Illingworth, C. (1964) *Babies and Young Children. A Guide for Parents*, London: Churchill Livingstone

Jackson, B. (1984) *Fatherhood*, London: Allen and Unwin

McKee, L. and O'Brien, M. (1982) *The Father Figure*, London: Tavistock Publications

Newsons, Janet and Elizabeth (1993) *Patterns of Infant Care in an Urban Community*: Pelican

Russell, B (1929) *Marriage and Morals*, London: George Allen and Unwin Ltd

Chapter 4

YOUNG PEOPLE'S ATTITUDES TO FATHERHOOD

Margaret O'Brien and Deborah Jones

Introducing the project *Inter-generational Perceptions of Fatherhood*

In this chapter, findings from a new project on fatherhood – *Inter-generational Perceptions of Fatherhood* – will be presented. The first phase of the project has focused on young people's attitudes to fatherhood. A central aim of the study has been to examine the meaning of fatherhood for contemporary children and their parents, both the public and private faces of fatherhood.

The study has been influenced by the observation that whilst the public, formal authority and power of fathers has declined in most western societies over the last century (described by some as the demise of patriarchy) at a private, relational level the picture is much more confusing and complex. In any one day one may hear about, see or personally experience diverse forms of fathering – from men in the local park carrying their babies in slings discussing feeding and sleeping practices, to men who find it difficult to fit in any time with their children and have little knowledge of their children's interests never mind food preferences. It appears that different models of fatherhood and fathering are being negotiated in the home, in the work-place and more widely across generations.

The 1980s debate in America and Europe on the "new man" signalled a significant break with past models of fatherhood and opened new sets of socially sanctioned ways of fathering. Being close, caring and emotionally committed to children became possible indeed desirable attributes of fathering (O'Brien, 1992). With these new possibilities came additional responsibilities and obligations over and above basic financial provision for the family unit.

During the same time period, however, there has been an apparent retreat by some men from taking emotional and financial responsibility for children. Research and social commentary has pointed to men's apparent flight from familial commitment following parenthood and after divorce (Bertaux and Delcroix, 1992). A growing number of children are being reared in households where their biological fathers are marginal or absent figures. This tendency has been described as a move towards "families without fatherhood" (e.g. Dennis and Erdos, 1992) or fragile fatherhood (Jensen, 1993).

It seems that in contemporary western societies, close and distant fatherhood models are developing alongside each other – or as some have put it "the good and bad father". What is lacking in the current debate in the UK is new empirical data on fatherhood and fathering styles in contemporary families and households by which to evaluate these competing claims. Still less is known about children's perspectives on fatherhood. We are hoping that our study will help fill this gap in knowledge.

The project itself is in two stages. The first stage has been a survey of young people's attitudes to family life, with a particular emphasis on their views on the responsibilities of fatherhood and their relationship with their own fathers (the father in their own lives rather than the father "out there"). Stage two will be a qualitative interview study of a sub-sample of the survey sample where family issues can be explored in more depth with the young people and their parents.

Respondents were recruited from six of the eight secondary state schools in an East London borough to represent the typical socio-economic profile of the area. Four class groups of mixed ability were selected from the third and fifth forms of each school. The children completed a questionnaire in the classroom and a daily diary for one week at home. Areas covered by the questionnaire were extensive, incorporating many aspects of the children's family relationships, social and educational circumstances as well as their attitudes to fatherhood, gender roles and family life. The diary was open-ended but included direct questions on the daily amount of time spent with parents and associated activities. This paper will concentrate on the survey data.

The young people

The average age of the young people was 14 years and 9 months. The gender balance was slightly in favour of boys, reflecting the local situation for this age group: 45% of the sample were girls and 55% were boys. The majority (83%) of the children, were white British, 9% were Asian and 5% Black British/Afro-Caribbean (the remaining 5% included children of European, Chinese or Arab origin). Whilst respondents predominately lived in two parent households, only 68% were still living with both their natural birth parents: 14% lived in step-families, mainly of the step-father type (12% step-father and 2% step-mother); 12% lived in lone mother households and 4% in lone father households. The remaining children lived with other guardians or with foster parents.

Over three-quarters of fathers (79%) and nearly two-thirds of mothers (62%) were in paid employment, lower than the national rates for this family life stage: 74% of economically active fathers were in full-time employment and 37% of mothers, the remainder being in part-time employment. Over the last fifteen years the area has seen a decline in the manufacturing sector and an increase in service sector employment, particularly for women. Whilst these trends were reflected in the sample, the most common male occupation was still in the skilled manual work category. The most common female occupation was in skilled non-manual work.

In comparison to London-wide standards, parental educational qualification levels were low: only 6% of fathers and 5% of mothers had a diploma, degree or higher degree.

In summary, these mainly white young people lived in predominately two parent households, but with a third having experienced some form of parental change since birth. A majority of parents were in employment, more fathers than mothers, in what might be summarized as predominately working-class occupations. Few parents were educationally qualified.

Attitudes to fatherhood

As was mentioned earlier, one of the objectives of the survey was to ascertain children's view on the duties, responsibilities and rights of contemporary fathers. Key aspects of contemporary fatherhood were examined including: attendance at childbirth; Paternity Leave; contact and economic support after divorce; perceptions of fathers' roles in families; and involvement in domestic duties.

Attendance at child-birth

Fathers' attendance at the birth of their children was an early indicator of what might be seen as new fatherhood and indeed the modern couple. By the early 1980s, over 70% of births were attended by fathers in contrast to the 1950s when the proportion was of the order of 10% (Lewis, Newson and Newson, 1982), called by Lorna McKee (1980) "the silent revolution". Research suggested that women were primary motivators in this change. Many contemporary fathers may now feel attendance is more a normative requirement rather than a voluntary act, but that is another issue. Children were asked whether they thought fathers should be present at the birth of their child and to give reasons for their views.

The results indicated that an overwhelming majority of children (95%) felt that fathers should be present. Table 1 shows the range of reasons offered as to why fathers should be present: just over 40% felt that fathers should be present to support mothers and share the responsibility: "to help the mother through it"; "to give support from the start". The second most frequently mentioned reason was that it was a father's right to be present. This accounted for 28% of the responses. Typical comments include: "because they made the baby they should have a right to be there"; "because it's their child too so it is only fair that if they wish they should be

Table 1. Reasons for attendance at birth (percent)

Support mother	42
Father's right	28
Bonding	21
Gain experience practical	3
Individual choice	3
Help with medical	0.5
Other	2.5

present"; "because it's father's child too not only mother's". Themes of ownership and paternity were dominant in these responses.

We have summarised the third most common response as bonding. Indeed some children mentioned this word themselves: "as they would see their new born child as soon as it is born – bonding"; "to see his child first".

Only a minority of children felt the father should not be present, expressing indifference or giving no reason or being concerned that the experience might be too horrific for fathers to bear – "a horrible sight" as one child commented. It appears therefore that attendance at a child's birth is generally expected of contemporary fathers, at least from this sample of young people.

Men's access to Paternity Leave

Debates about the legitimacy and indeed the necessity of Paternity Leave have been on-going in family policy circles since the 1970s (Bell, McKee and Priestley, 1983; Moss, 1993). But what do children think about Paternity Leave? In the question they were told that employed mothers can take paid time off after the birth of a baby (for information, as informal questioning suggested that children had little knowledge of this provision) and were asked whether employed fathers should be able to take paid time off work too during this period and to give reasons for their opinion.

A majority (70%), although not as large as for being present at the birth, felt that fathers should have access to paid Paternity Leave. There was a slight tendency for girls to be more in favour than boys. The predominant reason given (52%), and slightly more often by girls than boys, was to assist the mother and share the responsibility of looking after the baby: "because the mother may not be able to cope with looking after the baby and house"; "to help their wife cope with the birth and get sorted out". The second most frequent set of responses (22%) emphasised that it was a father's right to care for his child at this time; some even mentioned 'equal opportunities'. Boys were slightly more likely to give this reason (Table 2).

Table 2. Reasons for taking paternity leave (percent)

Assist mother	52
Father's right	22
Get to know baby	20
In case of mother's absence	2
Working mother	0.5
Other	3.5

About a third (30%) of the sample were of the opinion that fathers should not have Paternity Leave. The main reason for this view was the feeling that a father is required to earn money at this time (38%): "because there would be no money coming in for the baby". These children seemed to disregard the possibility, stated in the question, that Paternity Leave would be paid. The second most common reason as to why men should not have Paternity Leave (29%) was the view that only mothers required a rest at this time, not fathers: "they [fathers] have not just been through a painful birth they just stood there and watched". Others felt that caring for a baby only required one person or was primarily a mother's responsibility – "it's a lady's job" – and that father "might be a pain and get under her feet" (Table 3).

It is informative to compare these responses to one of the few UK surveys of adult men's attitudes to Paternity Leave conducted in the early 1980s – albeit with men interviewed 6-8 weeks after the birth of their child (Bell, McKee and Priestley, 1983). The overwhelming majority (91%) were in favour of some form of leave (of 1-2 weeks duration) and only 6% thought it should be unpaid. 50% thought full pay would be appropriate and 26% thought basic pay fair. Although to my knowledge there has been no systematic UK research since, it is clear that men as a social group have not been lobbying for

Table 3. Reasons fathers should not take paternity leave (percent)

Fathers need to earn money	38
Only mother requires rest	29
Only one person required	14
Mother's responsibility	13
Other	5

Paternity or Parental Leave. It may well be, however, that the next generation of fathers, of which these children will be part, may be more active in this area: women because they demand male support and men because they want the opportunity/right to spend time with their babies.

Fatherhood after divorce

With the increase in divorce there has been a growing concern about the role of fathers in post-divorce child care and about the nature of their involvement with children. We focused on two issues: whether fathers should be expected to contribute financially to the welfare of their children after divorce; and whether fathers, if they left home, should still be able to have contact with their children.

Again, the great majority (96%) felt that fathers should continue to support their children financially after divorce (showing full endorsement of at least the underlying sentiment of the Child Support Act). The most frequently mentioned reason given for financial support after divorce (55%) was that it was seen as a continuing part of a father's responsibilities: "he's still their dad", "because it is his child he should still support the child". The importance of financially assisting mothers was highlighted by a second group of respondents (41%): "because the mother wouldn't be able to cope", "the mother may only be working part-time and extra money could help". Only 4% per cent of the sample felt that fathers should not be obliged to financially contribute to their children after divorce and all but two of these twenty children were boys (a gender difference that was statically significant). Their predominant reason was that a divorced father was no longer part of the family and may indeed have another family to support (Table 4).

Table 4. Reasons fathers should financially support children after divorce (percent)

Father's responsibility	55
Assist mother	41
Father's right	2
Other	2

There was a similarly overwhelming proportion of children (97%) who felt that fathers should still have contact with their children after divorce. The children used the language of rights rather than responsibilities and obligations to justify their responses. Nearly half of the children (44%), significantly more boys than girls, stressed fathers' rights : "they should be able to if he wants, because its his child as well and he has a right to have contact", "he has a right to see them". Over a third of the children (39%), significantly more girls than boys, emphasised children's rights to continuing access to a father: "the children might not have done nothing to cause the divorce so why should they loose their father?" The continuing roles and responsibilities of fathering after divorce were mentioned by a minority (10%): "unless he has abused the child he should be allowed visits because it is only fair that he can give his guidance too" (Table 5).

Table 5. Reasons fathers should have contact with children after divorce (percent)

Father's right	44
Children's right	39
Father's responsibility	10
Other	7

Early results suggest that this predominately working class group of young people appear to endorse a modern "new father" model. Their model of fatherhood is of the emotionally involved, participative father who should be present at the birth of his children, take Paternity Leave, share many domestic duties with the mother (a further finding not detailed here) and continue to be in contact with and economically contribute to children's welfare after a divorce. When asked directly about what fathers should do in families these young people construct fatherhood as central to the emotional and material dimensions of family life.

Three main expectations of fathers emerge: economic provision; care and love; and involvement in the domestic life of families (Table 6). There were indications that perceptions of fatherhood were gendered. Girls were slightly more likely to emphasise fathers' emotionally supportive roles and boys the

Table 6. What should fathers do? (percent)

Earn money	34
Care and spend time	27
Domestic activities	25
Support (unspecified)	5
Model for child	4
Protect	2
Other	3

'rights' dimension (that is, rights of access after divorce, rights to be at the birth of their children, Paternity Leave rights) and economic provision.

Relationships with own fathers

As we have already mentioned, the first stage of the project was also concerned with children's relationships with their own resident fathers/step-fathers and non-resident fathers. For the purposes of this paper results on two aspects are summarized below: fathers' actual involvement in household domestic duties and use of father as confidante.

Father's involvement in household domestic duties

Children were asked about their **preferred** and **actual** allocation pattern for seven routine domestic tasks (shopping, cooking the evening meal, doing the evening dishes, household cleaning, washing and ironing clothes, repairing household equipment and organising household money and bills). Response categories ranged from "mainly men" through to "mainly children".

The majority favoured some form of sharing between the parents on most tasks. But when these attitudes are compared to reported reality there is a different picture. Sharing between parents was reported to take place in a minority of cases. It was the predominant response for only one domestic activity, organising household bills, and the second most common response in one instance – household shopping. Instead, according to the children, mothers took main responsibility for all remaining duties, except household repairs which remained the province of fathers (Table 7).

Table 7. Proportions of parents reported to share household
duties (percent)

Organising household money and bills	41
Household shopping	29
Evening meal	17
Evening dishes	16
Household cleaning	13
Washing and ironing clothes	10
Repairing household equipment	8

Reported father involvement and sharing increased when
mothers were in full-time employment (for shopping, evening
meal, evening dishes, cleaning, washing and ironing clothes)
and less strongly when fathers were unemployed (for shopping,
evening meal). This mismatch between ideals and reported
reality has been found by most adult surveys of domestic
division of labour and is supported here when the child's
viewpoint is considered.

Father as confidante

Emotional closeness is constructed as an important aspect of
modern fatherhood. We were interested therefore in the extent
to which children turned to fathers when they had personal
troubles and worries. Table 8 shows the proportions of children
who report talking to father first for various personal worries.
Other response categories included mother, friend of opposite
sex, friend of same sex, other person or no-one.

Children were asked about nine separate worries: progress
at school, problems with friends, problems with mother,
problems with father, self-confidence, progress at sports,
personal appearance, homework and money. As Table 8
indicates fathers were chosen as the first port of call by a
minority of children. In general mothers were the most popular
choice, followed by a friend of the same sex, a response found
also by Brannen et al (1994). However, fathers were the most
frequently mentioned person for three of the nine areas: money,
difficulties with mother and sport.

Boys were more likely to turn to their fathers first and
daughters to mothers. This gender pattern was also found when

Table 8. Father as main confidante (percent)

Money	44
Problems with mother	38
Progress at sports	31
Homework	23
Progress at school	17
Self-confidence	11
Problems with friends	10
Problems with father	5
Personal appearance	5

joint activities between parents and child were considered. Children were asked about the most favourite thing they liked doing with their fathers. Going out and doing things together related to leisure was the most common response (26% of sample), particularly from boys. Mothers were especially liked for "talking about things that matter" (38%), particularly by girls who were also most likely to enjoy this with their fathers.

It appears that boys and girls tended to use fathers and mothers differently and there was evidence that this pattern worked better for boys than girls. Girls were more dissatisfied than boys with the amount of time fathers gave them and were more likely to feel that their fathers did not understand them. Only 23% of girls but 44% of boys felt that their fathers understood them very well. A benevolent, slightly remote father appeared to be more satisfactory for the boys in this sample. (There were however variations linked to family type in that step fathers were perceived by both boys and girls as less understanding and lone fathers more understanding).

For those children who wanted their parents to spend more time with them, we asked what might help fathers and mothers to be able to do this. The most common response was for mothers and fathers to spend less time at work. This was most frequently mentioned for children who had parents who worked full-time: "if he did less days and nights at work he would want to see me more", "if we could do more things together", "if we could sit and talk", "if she did less hours at work I would see her more often".

Conclusion

The responsibilities of fatherhood, as described by this generational group, are in line with the family man of a modern symmetrical/egalitarian family where fathers are expected to be participative and emotionally involved with children. They are certainly not expected to be the rulers or the all-powerful family member or indeed the disciplinarian. However, when children's reported reality is contrasted against their normative expectations, fathers do not appear as central as mothers in everyday family life and a substantial minority of children, particularly daughters, are not satisfied with this discrepancy.

Compared to mothers, fathers are less likely to be used as confidantes at times of worry and are less involved in the domestic routine of households. There are suggestions though of a special father-son dimension in families centred around leisure and "non-shopping going-out". This will be explored further in our analysis of the diaries and during the second stage of the project when respondents from both generations are to be interviewed.

There is a degree of mismatch, therefore, between attitudes/values and reported behaviour concerning the responsibilities of fatherhood. As Finch and Mason (1993) have shown, actual behaviour cannot be "read off" from family values reported in surveys. They suggest that the enactment of family responsibilities can be seen as a series of "negotiated commitments" from actors in different structural positions, subject to individual variation but developing within specific normative guidelines. What needs to be explored further in the qualitative stage of this research is the extent to which children, particularly daughters, in the context of a companionate and nurturant fatherhood model, manage the everyday emotional and physical absences of fathers.

References

Bell, C., McKee, L. and Priestley, K. (1983) *Fathers, Childbirth and Work*, Manchester: Equal Opportunities Commission

Bertaux, D. and Delcroix, C. (1992) "Where have all the Daddies Gone?", in U. Bjornberg (ed.) *European Parents in the 1990s: Contradictions and Comparisons*, New Brunswick: Transaction

Brannen, J., Dodd, K., Oakley, A. and Storey, P. (1994) *Young People, Health and Family Life*, Buckingham: Open University Press

Carlsen, S. and Larsen, J. (1993) (eds.) *The Equality Dilemma: Reconciling Working Life and Family Life, viewed in an Equality Perspective*, Copenhagen: Danish Equal Status Council

Census Borough Profile (1993) Borough of Barking and Dagenham

Danish Ministry of Social Affairs (1993) (ed.) *Fathers in Families of Tomorrow, Proceedings of a Conference held in Copenhagen June 1993*, Copenhagen: The Ministry of Social Affairs

Dennis, N. and Erdos, G. (1992) *Families without Fatherhood*, London: The IEA Health and Welfare Unit

Ferri, E. (1994) "Parenting–Sociological Perspectives", paper presented to an ESRC Seminar on *Parenting in the 1990s* held in London, February 1994

Finch, J. and Mason, J. (1993) *Negotiating Family Responsibilities*, London: Routledge

Jensen, A.M. (1993) "Fathers and Children – The Paradox of Closeness and Distance", in Danish Ministry of Social Affairs (ed.) *Fathers in Families of Tomorrow*, Proceedings of a Conference held in Copenhagen June 1993, Copenhagen: The Ministry of Social Affairs

Lewis, C., Newson, E., and Newson, J. (1982) "Father Participation through childhood and its relation to Career Aspirations and Delinquency", in N. Beail and J. McQuire (eds) *Fathers: Psychological Perspectives*, London: Junction Books

McKee, L. (1980) 'Fathers and Childbirth – Just hold my hand', *Health Visitor* Vol 53

Moss, P. (1993) "Strategies to Promote Fathers' involvement in the care and upbringing of their children: Placing leave arrangements in a wider context", in Danish Ministry of Social Affairs (ed.) *Fathers in Families of Tomorrow, Proceedings of a Conference held in Copenhagen June 1993*, Copenhagen: The Ministry of Social Affairs

O'Brien, M. (1992) "Changing Conceptions of Fatherhood", in U. Bjornberg (ed.) *European Parents in the 1990s: Contradictions and Comparisons*, New Brunswick: Transaction Publications

Why every son needs his father figure

LESSON FOR LIFE: The presence of a caring, affectionate father gives children the best start

P OOR, underestimated fathers are at long last being appreciated. Psychologists, who have for so long paid them scant regard, are finally recognising that fathers have a role to play that is crucial not just for their own children, but for society in general.

It is ironic that it should happen now, when a lot of men could be forgiven for wondering whether

by Dr JENNY ......

adolescents' relationships with both their parents when they were young, are more likely now to be arrested, have problems, love more

and stay away in fact the father. Then in the way they want to develop themselves, may soon to understand an early road to what they are

We all agree ....

Chapter 5

FATHERS IN THE MEDIA
An analysis of newspaper coverage of fathers

Trefor Lloyd

THE media is an important source of insight into current ideas about fathers and fatherhood, as well as being a powerful force in shaping those ideas. For example, a study by a Swedish researcher examined how the image of the Swedish father has changed through an examination of magazines, advertisements and textbooks between 1934 and 1988. In the 1930s, the Swedish father was typically shown in a relaxed "weekend" atmosphere, then as time passed began to be portrayed more often as a "working day" parent. Recently, fathers have moved into areas such as household work and child care. Over time, however, the definition of the "good father" was consistently grounded in middle class values (Hagstro, 1991). A similar exercise has been conducted for American fathers, this time using newspaper cartoons. Until the 1970s, these cartoons presented fathers as incompetent child caretakers, but during the 1970s there were signs of a shift: fathers began to appear as potentially useful, although failing to achieve their potential (Day and Mackey, 1986).

During June 1994, I was asked by the European Commission Network on Childcare and Other Measures to Reconcile Employment and Family Responsibilities to carry out an analysis of the coverage of fathers and fatherhood, mothers and motherhood, parents and parenthood and men as carers in ten daily and ten Sunday papers[1]. This was part of a larger exercise monitoring newspapers in seven Member States in the European Union (for the final report of this exercise, see Deven,

---

[1] The newspapers monitored were the *Sun*, *Daily* and *Sunday Mirror*, *Daily Mail* and *Mail on Sunday*, *Daily* and *Sunday Express*, *Daily* and *Sunday Telegraph*, *Daily Record*, *Today*, the *Financial Times*, the *Sunday Times*, the *Guardian*, the *Independent* and *Independent on Sunday*, *Sunday Sport*, *Observer* and the *People*.

1995). The EU has for some time recognised that reconciliation of employment and family responsibilities is an important condition for achieving one of its policy objectives – gender equality in the labour market. Moreover, it has also recognised for some time that reconciliation requires more equal sharing of these family responsibilities between men and women. The EU therefore has an agenda which includes fathers, employment and caring for children; the monitoring exercise was intended, in part, to see whether this subject was also on the public agenda in Member States, at least as revealed by newspapers.

In this chapter, I will concentrate on one part of the monitoring exercise: the coverage of fathers and fatherhood. In all, over the four week period, 280 newspapers were scanned and there were 234 items relating to fathers and fatherhood – more than mothers and motherhood (165 items) or parents and parenthood (119). News and feature articles comprised over three-quarters of all of the items, with two-thirds of these being news items; the rest were a mix of photo features, letters, comment, adverts and so on.

Sarah Heatley with her children, Jack and Nina

Doctor strangled his two children

By Colin Wright

A DOCTOR strangled his young son and daughter and then jumped to his death from a block of flats after learning his estranged wife was seeing another man, an inquest in Sheffield was told yesterday.

Dr Sukhdev Sandhu, 35, killed Nina, four, and Jack, three, wrapping their bodies in quilts in the cellar of his rented home in Sheffield before ringing an undertaker friend and saying: "Come

their father could ever hurt them is unbelievable but that he could end their lives is far beyond comprehension. He proved himself to be the cruellest of bullies."

Mr Christopher Dorries, the coroner, heard that Sandhu and his wife had married in 1988 after meeting at Roehampton Hospital, where they both worked, before moving to a Derbyshire village from where the GP commuted to his practice

Family wiped out by young father's jealous rampage

Daily Mail Reporter

A VILLAGE was in mourning last night for a 'perfect' family of four wiped out by jealousy.

Carpenter Mark Bradley apparently shot his wife then gassed himself and his two young children after love affairs tore their marriage apart.

The couple had returned only a week ago from a holiday in Turkey where

young lives. It's dreadful.' Neighbour Pat Upperton told how she last saw fair-haired Daniel on Tuesday. She said: 'He saw me and shouted, "Pat, I love you".

'They were lovely children. Mark was a marvellous carpenter and in the house there was a beautiful grandfather clock that he had made.

'They were a happy couple but lately something didn't seem quite right and suddenly Donna was often missing. I had a feeling something was amiss.'

By far the largest group of items (38) were stories of **Fathers as Monsters** – most of these either killed, abused or bullied those that were closest to them. Over half involved "tennis dads', provoked by Mary Pierce's withdrawal from Wimbledon. How long a story runs seems to have a major influence on what is uncovered and how the people involved are perceived. With Mary Pierce, her father started the months as the "dad from hell" and ended it as a father who tried too hard! While the language or actions usually suggested a monster, most of the feature articles asked (or guessed) why the fathers took the actions they did – he was "depressed/provoked/etc." When the item was news (especially when it was the tabloids), usually the basic "monster" facts were given and no reasons why.

There were a number of other themes that recurred during the month:

Famous people – in particular, this was a major theme with a number of tabloids. It took a number of forms. "Looking Good as Dads" produced 25 photographs of famous fathers with their children. The sportsmen in these photographs usually suggested the strong and gentle – most were big men with very small children. Photographs of Prince Charles with his sons seemed to present a contrast to the perception of him as a poor husband and father which the media had been presenting. "Reflections on Famous Dads" by their children produced 8 items, and the tone tended to be negative. Lord Olivier's son wrote that his father's "work took all his creativity; when he came home, he wasn't a giving person". He has setup a support group for men whose fathers were distant. A D-Day related feature on Montgomery described him as "cold, remote and ruthlessly critical towards his son, who never had a conversation with him about emotions" and also mentioned that his son does not talk about emotions to his son. The article concluded that he was a "great general, lousy father". "Reflections from famous sons and daughters" on their fathers produced 11 items, and the tone again was mainly negative, reflecting abandonment and monster behaviour – although sons come across as more unforgiving than daughters.

Fathers who Changed their Behaviour Because of their Children (11 items) – this theme highlights an important dimension of fathers" relationships with their children which is still relatively unexplored. The items were however on the whole about famous men, "humanized" by their children. Don Johnson (actor) checked into a "booze clinic" 48 hours after nearly killing his son in a car crash when he had been drinking. Eddie Murphy, another actor, is "more interested in nappies than parties these days", "marriage and fatherhood have mellowed the star". Eric Clapton (musician) had become a born-again Christian: three years after the death of his four-year-old son, he was so grief-stricken, it made him "go off the edge of the world". Jeremy Bates puts his success at Wimbledon down to baby Joshua: "I've realized that there are other things apart

from tennis". Under the heading, "He ain't heavy, he's my father", was the story of Hannah who, having looked at her 22 stone father and a picture of him as a slender teenager, said "I want you to look like that again": 18 months later, he had lost 10 stone and become Slimming World Man of the Year.

Fathers as influential in children's lives (8 items) – one study suggested that strict fathers cause stress, particularly in sons'

THE DAILY TELEGRAPH

Strict fathers can cause stress in their sons' careers

MEN who find it difficult to get on with their boss were often brought up by strict fathers, the British Psychological Society said yesterday.

The Society said the influence of fathers is central to the way in which children, particularly boys, relate to other people in adult life.

Its report, based on the work of three psychologists, suggests the influence of fathers is greater than previously supposed and casts doubt on the prospects of the increasing number of children brought up by single mothers.

Dr Jenny Firth-Cozens, of Leeds University, followed the progress of 500 doctors from the time they were medical students 10 years ago to their present positions as GPs and hospital doctors.

She found the long hours worked by hospital doctors did not explain the stress some of them experienced as well as their early relationships with their mother and father.

"The main predictors of whether they now suffer from stress or depression is how self-critical they were as

By David Fletcher
Health Services Correspondent

students and the extent to which they saw their relationship with their mother as guilty and anxious," she said.

She found the influence of the doctors' fathers exerted a crucial influence on the way they related to their hospital bosses.

"Those who find their relationship particularly stressful are those who, 10 years earlier, reported their fathers to be powerful, critical, strict and hard to please, and their own relationship to their fathers as guilty and anxious."

Dr Firth-Cozens said another study which followed the progress of a group of five-year-olds for 36 years found those with less affectionate relationships with one or both parents at the age of five were less likely to have married only once at the age of 41, less likely to have children, or to have done well in their jobs. They also had fewer friends and poorer mental health.

"This was particularly

important in terms of father-son relationships at five. Such a study shows the importance of what is paid lip service to but not always achieved — an affectionate family life with both parents."

She said the studies showed that fathers were more central, especially to the lives of their sons, than was previously realised and the implications for children brought up by single mothers were "grim."

Dr Peter Stratton, director of the Leeds Family Therapy and Research Centre, said it was important for children in single-parent families to know something of their father.

Children who had plenty of positive information about their father, even though he was missing, were less likely to experience problems. Adopted children were also helped by knowing about their parents.

"It is important that the children can be reassured that although their biological parents may have made mistakes and been unable to cope with parenthood at the time, they were not monsters but ordinary, struggling people."

careers. Another study found that absent fathers led to children (especially sons) being less academic, more prone to absenteeism, doing less homework, and being less sociable and less confident. The article reporting this study stressed that fathers needed to be caring, affectionate, playful, encouraging and able to rejoice in their children's success:

> *Our sons are in danger of growing up believing that the boyish things that come naturally to them are in some way peculiar and unhealthy – and have a lack of role-models... Whatever happened to the patriarch, the transmitter of moral authority? He seems to have shifted into a faintly ridiculous person...[There are now] three kinds of Dad, the active new dad, the detached CSA dad, and the humorous card dad as idiot... Fathers are often perceived as remote, absent or neglectful. We are not so very distant from the time we simply expected them to bring in the money and carve the Sunday joint.*

Men as Sperm Donors (9 items) – this theme mainly focused on some form of artificial insemination. For example, a widow asked for sperm to be removed from her husband hours after he

Tennis star quits in torment over father

He vowed to 'create a spectacle' at Wimbledon

BY MARGARET HUSSEY, RICHARD EVANS AND MIKE SWAIN

TENNIS star Mary Pierce sensationally pulled out of Wimbledon last night in fear of her father.

The 19-year-old is terrified her estranged father — a schizophrenic and convicted criminal — would turn up to watch her.

Jim Pierce, 58, has stalked Mary across the globe. He has been ban-

shattered at losing the opportunity to play at Wimbledon and the whole event had been a nightmare.

In a prepared statement issued last night, she said: "For reasons far beyond my control, I have decided not to participate in the most prestigious and traditional tournament in the world.

"Without a doubt they clearly indicated that my absence and withdrawal would serve the best interest

had died, saying "I want a piece of him to live on"; a pioneering technique was reported where a single sperm is injected directly into the centre of each egg, which had helped a couple conceive; and a woman wanted to keep custody of five frozen embryos as part of a divorce settlement. A rather different story concerned a man who had had a vasectomy and whose wife subsequently became pregnant, he accused her of being a "slut', beat up his

AMAZING BABY No 1

THE WAY THEY WERE: Pam and Manny Maresca

I'll get pregnant by dead husband

A WIDOW is hoping to have a baby by using sperm taken from her husband – hours AFTER he died from car-crash injuries.

best friend because he was convinced he was the father, then discovered that his severed tubes had joined up!

The Child Support Agency (9 items) – the most notable point about this theme was the relatively few items during June; at other times in 1994, the number would have been much higher, reflecting the high prominence given to the issue of the financial responsibility of absent fathers.

Fathers' Rights and Responsibilities (8 items) – a letter was printed from a man who had discovered that he had made a second woman pregnant, the other being his fiancee, whom he will marry in three months. The advice given was that:

> As a father, you will need to be financially responsible for the children... if you do not use condoms, then you will make babies... you must take responsibility for your action: your fiancee needs to know what you are like.

The wife of Jean Alesi (motor racing driver) had "begged him not to shun the baby daughter that wrecked their marriage". He left the marriage in January, saying he was not ready for fatherhood and the new responsibilities that came with it: "I don't want a child while I am driving – I risk my life – it would be irresponsible".

Distressed and Violent Fathers (7 items) – these items reflected the form in which many men show their feelings, when they are angry, upset or hurt. One case reported involved a "distraught father [who] tried to attack the killer of his teenage daughter in the court of appeal". In another example, a man was cleared of assault in court for hitting his seven-year-old son with a belt after the children had painted on a carpet; the court was told that his parents had had to put up with five years of disturbed behaviour. Newspapers tended to be sympathetic towards the men involved – as were the courts.

There was only one article that looked at, or even referred to black men. The opening quote, from Darcus Howe (TV presenter/commentator/activist) was "I am a West Indian. That means I make children all the time". The article suggested a gulf between black women, better educated and expecting more from men than black men can offer, and black men, who had

Man cleared after hitting son who painted carpets

By Nigel Bunyan

A FATHER was justified in hitting his seven-year-old son on the bottom with a belt after he awoke to find the boy had covered walls, carpets, furniture and clothes with white paint, a jury decided yesterday.

The 24-year-man, who was cleared of assault, snapped after enduring five years of disturbed behaviour from the child, Mold Crown Court was told.

In the past his son, who

this." He said he had tried everything from slapping to refusing to let him use his computer game or go on school trips. But nothing seemed to work. He had consulted a doctor, who prescribed sleeping drops, and later a child therapist.

Hitting him had been the "last resort", he said.

Mr Zia Chowdhury, defending, asked the jurors what they would have done had they awoken to such a

fewer breadwinning opportunities and often perceived black women as greedy and manipulative.

Finally, it is important to consider these themes on fathers and fatherhood alongside coverage of two other areas included in the monitoring study – employment and family life and men as carers for children. "Reconciliation of employment and family life" only produced 28 items in the month, and these mainly concerned cases involving the dismissal of pregnant women from the Armed Services and employment issues concerning women and children. References to men concentrated on the loss of male employment – "men on the scrap heap – raw economics rather than sexual politics have achieved that dream of the more extreme women's libbers, men are redundant and have little choice of work" – to the exclusion of any reference to the relationship between employment and children. "Men as carers for children" turned up a mere 8 items, which included allegations of rape and indecent assault against a male babysitter and male teacher, and the story of a male broadcaster who had smuggled a Bosnian orphan into this country.

Conclusions

There are a number of conclusions that can be drawn from this analysis:

1. The most striking aspect is the preoccupation of most of the media with the rich and famous and personal interest stories. Throughout the month, there were only 14 features looking at the broader issues relating to fathers and fatherhood.

2. There is a very limited debate within the media about fathers (and also, more generally, about men and caring for children). What debate there is focuses on the changing role of men as breadwinners. Items either concentrated on men who were working (the rich and famous included) and their role in the family as leisure time, or the effects on fathers, mothers and children when they are not in work. A broader discussion about women as workers and mothers (and the effects of work on them and their children) was much more apparent. However, while mothers trying to look after their children and work were quickly criticised for not doing the two successfully, men were not even expected to do them well – the issue of how to reconcile employment and family life was not on the agenda for them.

3. Men with children and without wives were a focus of some debate. Both were viewed on the whole sympathetically (unlike single mothers) and in need of help.

4. Most of the newspaper items saw fathers as either heroes or villains. Monster stories were as popular as the glossy rich and famous men looking good with their children. Fathers did heroic things, or side-stepped their responsibilities, but very little in between.

5. There was very little comment about what fathers are supposed to be, no guidance about how to be a father in the 1990s, with any pointers faltering after breadwinner and the general call on men to "take more responsibility". "Parenting" was seen as a function to be carried out on behalf of the state, while

"motherhood" was seen as a personal choice (and a necessity for fulfilment) and "fatherhood" as a responsibility.

6. Judged from the newspapers, issues concerning the sharing of family responsibilities between men and women, reconciliation of employment and family life for men as well as women and the role of men and fathers as carers have failed to establish themselves on the public agenda in Britain in the 1990s.

References

Day, R.D. and Mackey, W.C. (1986) "The role model of American fathers: an examination of a media myth', *Journal of Comparative Family Studies*, 17 (3), 371–388

Deven, F. (1995) *Men, Media and Childcare*, Brussels: European Commission Equal Opportunities Unit

Hagstro, L. (1991) "Den massmediale fadern: fadersrollen spegled i veckopress, reklam och larobocker genom femtio ar', *Nord-Nytt*, 44, 25–33

Chapter 6

WHEN WORKING MEN BECOME FATHERS

Søren Carlsen

Introduction

One of the most topical equal status issues in Denmark, and in the Nordic countries in general, is men's use of Parental Leave (see Footnote, page xvii of the Introduction for an explanation of Parental Leave and Paternity Leave). The reason is, primarily, that most fathers do not make use of their right to this long period of leave, which would enable them to spend time together with, and caring for, their very young children. There are several reasons why men's use of Parental Leave is so crucial to equal status.

In Denmark, an equal status strategy has long been adopted, the basis of which is the "dual breadwinner" family; both parents, if they want to be, should be part of the labour market. Following women's massive entry into the labour market, the need arose for Parental Leave schemes. But from an equal status point of view it is a problem if only the mother takes Parental Leave: women come to be seen as "difficult" labour, who are away from the labour market for long periods of time when they give birth to children. The equal status argument is that if fathers were to take a long period of leave as well, many equal status problems in the labour market would be solved. It should not, however, be forgotten that, though the introduction of Paternity and Parental Leave in Denmark in 1986 was a result primarily of equal status considerations, it is also desirable that fathers should take leave because it is good for children and for fathers themselves.

In this chapter I have chosen to focus on the issue of men's use of Parental Leave as it implies a significant departure from the approach of earlier generations to the role of the father. This issue also provides an illustrative example of some of the problems which arise when steps are taken politically to influence the position of men in the family. In the following sections, I present the results of a Nordic survey of men's use of Parental Leave, which I have just finished, and put forward seven proposals for initiatives which will make Parental Leave schemes more "father friendly" and therefore contribute to stimulating men's use of Parental Leave. By way of conclusion I shall comment on what lessons may be drawn from the Nordic efforts at promoting men's use of leave.

Danish leave arrangements

In Denmark, until recently the total leave period after the birth of the child has been 24 weeks: 14 weeks Maternity Leave, followed by 10 weeks Parental Leave which the parents may divide between them as they choose. In addition, the father is entitled to 2 weeks Paternity Leave during the first 14 weeks after the birth of the child. Parents taking leave receive a payment from public funds equivalent to unemployment benefit, which is on average approximately 45% of a male blue-collar worker's pay and approximately 55% of a female blue-collar worker's pay. Under their collective agreement all public sector employees are entitled to full pay in connection with all of these types of leave.

In addition, for the period 1994–1996 a special Childcare Leave scheme has been introduced on a trial basis (although similar to Parental Leave, this additional period is referred to, in Danish, as Childcare Leave to emphasise the benefit to the children; it is referred to below as "Childcare Leave", to distinguish it from the 10 week "Parental Leave" period). Under this trial scheme **each** parent is entitled to a further 6 months leave per child, which may be extended to 1 year per child subject to negotiation with the employer; this leave may be taken at any time until the child is eight years old. Parents taking this Childcare Leave receive a payment from public funds equivalent to 80% of unemployment benefits (in 1994, DKK2,035 per week, or about £240); local authorities may also supplement this payment, and in 1994 about two-thirds of local authorities chose to do so, paying on average DKK30,000 per year (or about £3,550)[1].

Approximately half of all Danish fathers now take the 2 weeks Paternity Leave. But only 3% have taken part of the 10 week Parental Leave period introduced in 1986. So far, however, fathers constitute about 9% of the users of the new Childcare Leave scheme.

What do we know about the Danish fathers who have used their right to take Parental Leave? They are more likely:

- to work in the public sector than the private sector;
- to have had intermediate or higher education;
- to work in workplaces where most of the workforce is female;
- to have a partner who is highly educated, has a strong commitment to the labour market and has a high salary.

In short, what emerges is a pattern showing that it is the so-called "A team" on the labour market – i.e. those who are well educated with permanent jobs and high income – who most often take Parental Leave; and that the relation of the mother to the labour market seems to play an important role.

A number of surveys have been conducted to identify the barriers which stop men using Parental Leave. They show that, broadly speaking, there are three main reasons why men do not make use of their right to Parental Leave:

- their workplace does not allow it;
- the mother wants to take the leave because she wants to breastfeed and recuperate (it should be remembered that Maternity Leave and Parental Leave together finish before the baby reaches six months);
- the family cannot afford it, since as a rule the family's loss of income is greater if the father takes leave than if

---

[1]The new Childcare Leave scheme proved very popular in 1994, its first year of operation. From 1995, it has been modified so that each parent is only entitled to 6 months leave if they take the leave while their child is under 12 months of age; otherwise the entitlement is reduced to 3 months per parent and the period subject to employer agreement is increased to 9 months. Payment is also reduced to 70% of unemployment benefit. Childcare Leave in this modified form is now permanent; it is no longer a trial scheme.

the mother does because the father earns more than the mother.

Some results from the survey *When Men Become Fathers*

In an attempt to cast more light on why men do not make more use of Parental Leave, the Danish Equal Status Council decided, in co-operation with the Nordic Council of Ministers, to conduct a survey of men's experiences of Parental Leave. I shall mention here some of the results which are relevant to the subject of this chapter (for a more detailed account, see Carlsen and Larsen, 1993).

- The approach of workplaces is, in general, favourable towards men taking 2 weeks Paternity Leave but less so towards the longer Parental Leave. Several of the interviewees suggested that taking Paternity Leave has now become the workplace norm.

- The survey shows that it is most difficult to be the first man at a workplace, or among the first men, wanting to use the opportunity of Parental Leave.

- In work environments characterised by direct competition among staff, men make less use of leave opportunities and the right of absence when the child is ill than men who work in places without any competition among staff. In places where staff work in autonomous groups on joint projects, the culture is one of greater solidarity, with men showing consideration for each other.

- Leave makes up only one part of men's absence from work when they have children. In the survey, a great number of fathers used holiday leave and time off in lieu of overtime to extend their Paternity Leave and as an extension of the Parental Leave taken by the mother; the survey showed absence from work ranging from 2 weeks to 5 months. Similarly, several of those interviewed changed working hours to permanent evening/night work in order to be with their children during the day.

These types of absence and planning of working hours out of consideration for care of the children are not recorded in any statistics, and show fathers are good at finding other solutions. They emphasise that Parental Leave statistics cannot be used as a yardstick of men's wish to be involved in childcare. The problem is, however, that these are individual solutions, which the strongest groups in the labour market are best able to obtain through negotiation.

- Once fathers return to work at the end of their leave, the workplace often seems to forget that they have continuing family responsibilities. Workplaces react negatively when men are no longer able to do much overtime, when they no longer want to work inconvenient hours, when they stay at home because the children are ill etc.

Proposals for making Parental Leave schemes more "father friendly"

The project *When Men Become Fathers* led to seven recommendations to make Parental Leave schemes more "father friendly" and to promote their use by men.

Proposal 1. Leave as a personal entitlement

Men's entitlement to leave, including economic compensation for the period of leave, should be an independent right and not linked to whether or not the mother is employed. If the father's access to leave and economic compensation while on leave is dependant on the mother's entitlement to leave, as is the case in Norway and Iceland, obstacles are created to society's acceptance of the father as a person who is important to the care of the child, and it becomes difficult to gain acceptance in society for men's use of leave.

Proposal 2. Time and length of leave

Men should have an individual right to at least:

- 1 month of leave after the birth of the child (Paternity Leave);
- 6 months leave after the child's sixth month (Parental/Childcare Leave).

It was a generally expressed wish among the interviewees in the survey that it ought to be possible to have 1 month of leave after the birth of a child to enable the family to find a new routine and for the father to have a real opportunity to participate in the care of the young child right from the beginning. The recommendation that fathers should have access to at least 6 months leave after the child's sixth month arises from the responses of fathers in the survey. According to them the question of whether they should have Parental Leave during the first six months after the birth of their child was never really discussed in the family, since in general mothers want to be at home during this period and it is taken for granted that this will be the arrangement.

Proposal 3. Leave scheme flexibility

The leave schemes ought to be flexible to make it possible to take part-time leave or to divide the leave into shorter periods. A Swedish survey in 1990 showed that 33% of the Swedish fathers who had taken a period of Parental Leave had used some form of flexibility (the Swedish Parental Leave scheme allows leave to be taken both part-time and divided into short blocks of time); in 1986 the corresponding figure was 24%. The survey showed that this flexibility mainly took the form of taking leave in short blocks of time (e.g. taking leave every other week or 2–3 days of leave a week so that the mother and the father take it in turns to stay home and go to work). Part-time leave (e.g. working reduced hours each day) was not used so often.

The survey further found that the men who took flexible leave experienced their leave in a more positive light than fathers who took one period of full-time leave, for example reporting much less social isolation.

Proposal 4. Leave divided up into quotas

In addition to the special Paternity Leave at the time of the birth of the child, Parental/Childcare Leave schemes ought to allow for a period of time reserved for the father, an entitlement which cannot be transferred to the mother. This would have two purposes. On the one hand pressure is brought to bear on the ather: if he does not take leave, the family loses the opportunity of having the period of leave in question (you "use it or lose it"). On the other hand, introducing a quota of leave for fathers is a signal to their workplaces that fathers must prioritise child care for a certain period of time. This means that a special quota of leave for men may help fathers who would like to take leave but encounter opposition from their superiors and colleagues.

Proposal 5. Economic compensation

There should be differentiated economic compensation, with higher payments for those periods of leave reserved exclusively for one of the parents and lower payments for periods when the parents may decide themselves which of them is to take the leave.

Proposal 6. Information

There should be a high level of information on men's access to Parental Leave including both general information and publicity campaigns and targeted initiatives aimed at men's workplaces as well as at new parents and parents-to-be.

Proposal 7. Networks for men on Parental Leave

Many fathers on Parental Leave feel a certain degree of social isolation, especially if they are on full-time leave for a long period of time. To counter this social isolation, special efforts should be made, for example by midwives and health visitors, to establish networks for fathers on leave.

If the seven recommendations are accepted, a Parental Leave scheme might look as follows:

- Leave reserved for the father (with a high level of economic compensation)
  - 1 month from the birth of the child (Paternity Leave);
  - 3 months Parental Leave.
- Leave reserved for the mother (with a high level of economic compensation)
  - 1 month prior to the birth of the child;

- 3 months Parental Leave immediately after the birth of the child.

• Leave where the parents themselves choose which of them is to take leave (with a lower level of economic compensation)
    - 6 months Parental Leave.

Experience gained from Nordic efforts to promote men's use of Parental Leave

By way of conclusion I should like to mention very briefly some of the Nordic experience gained from efforts to influence the role of men in the family.

In drawing up strategies for increasing men's involvement in child care, it is necessary to focus on men, i.e. on men's conditions in relation to work, children and the mothers of their children. The point of departure must be men and not women. Consider this example: must fathers necessarily take full-time Parental Leave because mothers, for natural reasons, need a period of full-time leave after having given birth? Offering only full-time leave is of course the ultimate equality solution to the problem as it means that children will prove as much of a "handicap" to men as to women. However, it is hardly conducive to men's use of Parental Leave.

Following from this point of departure, we have to accept that men are different. It sounds like a cliché, for we know from labour market research, social research and educational research how different men are. Nevertheless, in the efforts to involve men in child care, this is often forgotten. For example, in Denmark there is one type of leave. There is hardly any scope for flexibility; it must be taken full-time and in one block. However, it is common experience in Denmark, but also in Sweden, that certain groups of men, often those who represent the so-called "B-team" on the labour market, for various reasons practically never take Parental Leave. Attention needs to be given to developing schemes which would make it possible for these groups of men also to take Parental Leave.

Finally, a process is underway in which the priority men give to the care of children is increasing – both in terms of what they want and their willingness to act. In Sweden approximately half the fathers take some Parental Leave. But it has taken 20 years to reach this stage, despite the fact that much work has been done there about men's involvement with children and equal status. We must therefore accept that, in this field things take time.

References

Carlsen, S. and Larsen, J. (1993) *The Equality Dilemma: Reconciling Working Life and Family Life, viewed in an equality Perspective,* Copenhagen: Danish Equal Status Council

Chapter 7

IN CONCLUSION
What opportunities are open to fathers?

Charlie Lewis

Two interwoven themes stitch the papers in this book together into what appears to be a sturdy back cloth, against which we can develop an understanding of contemporary fatherhood. The first theme is that we are in a period of reassessment. Fatherhood seems to be under the public gaze and we do not fully approve of what we see. The second theme in these chapters is that attempts to change this image of fatherhood by incorporating men into the centre of family activity have shown that change is a difficult process to effect. It is suggested that the image of fatherhood is too tarnished easily to be polished up.

I see my task in this concluding chapter as being to unpick some of the threads of the arguments in the preceding chapters, so that we can explore their various layers more closely. By and large I have few points of disagreement with what are a stimulating set of contributions, which do fit together surprisingly well despite their diverse starting points. Nevertheless, for the sake of acting in accordance with what is expected of a discussant, I will position my discussion in contrast with the perspectives taken by the authors in this book.

The role of a discussant is not far removed from the position of fathers in most families. Fathers' inputs contrast with, or at least complement, the activities of other participants in the family life. Usually, but by no means exclusively (as Sean French's domestic arrangements may well illustrate), the man's role is limited to one of acting as "helper" to his partner in the business of caring for children and keeping a home going. Just why such an arrangement is adopted in most households appears complex. Terms like "tradition" and "socialisation" do not fully capture the process by which parents take up their respective responsibilities, since there are so many variations on parental themes and so many striking examples of people who develop lifestyles in order to show their parents that there are alternative ways of organising family life. In the 1970s, for example, men who took up highly involved domestic roles by living in communes were more likely to report that their own fathers had been work-centred to the degree of neglecting their families (Eiduson et al, 1982).

In contrast to many of the perspectives taken in this book I wish to stress that a **combination** of factors interact to produce parental sex roles. These include not only tradition and socialisation (what Oakley (1979) has termed men's "trained incapacity to share" – but also the external relations between the "family" and the outside world (e.g. the availability of extra-familial care, or the various pressures on family members in the work force) and relations between family members. On this latter point research on women's perspectives on fatherhood has suggested an ambivalence; a desire to see the father becoming more involved, coupled with feelings of wanting to preserve their control over the responsibilities of parenthood (Lamb & Oppenheim, 1989; Lewis, 1986). It is in the light of such dynamics that the middle four chapters might be examined critically, in their shared attempt to grapple with understanding contemporary images of fatherhood.

Images of fatherhood

Julie Smith produces an interesting selection of comments taken from parenting manuals. These certainly convey the ridicule which fathers have been exposed to and the neglect of men's capacity to care for others. However, I take issue with her analysis on two points.

The first is her claim that fathers were overlooked before World War II. I disagree. Not only have fathers been mentioned in much parenting literature throughout this century (see e.g. La Rossa et al., 1991), but it is clear from the essays on men and fatherhood by William Cobbett (1828–32) that for over 160 years fathers have been subject to the same types of critical scrutiny as they receive today.

The second, more substantive, point is that it seems important to link what is written about fathers (and families more generally), in terms of the complexity of issues which I have described above. Father–child relationships are influenced by a variety of events. For example, it seems hardly a coincidence that fatherhood was treated lightheartedly in post-war texts, with many men returning to families they hardly knew and social pressures to promote women's domesticity so that veteran soldiers could have a job to reward them for their wartime duties. My point is that we need to know more about why fathers are depicted in particular ways rather than just the descriptions of a small selection of texts.

Angela Phillips presents a disturbing account of paternal involvement in families. Rogue male elephants do not only posture, they inflict brutal damage on those they come into contact with. She questions whether fathers are capable of rising to the challenges of parenthood and calls for a revolution amongst men to meet such challenges. While it is clear that some men do abrogate their responsibilities, particularly after parents separate, I am not convinced that Angela Phillips' analysis applies to more than a few. Even in such extreme cases it is not completely clear that the responsibility be should be charged solely to "errant" fathers. For example, the research by Edward Kruk (1993) suggests that fathers who "disengage" from their parental responsibilities after divorce report having been **more** involved with their children before the separation. The lesson to learn is that we have to theorise more deeply about why some fathers become physically or psychologically absent from the family and why others take a very active role.

My only comment on Sean French's analysis is that while it was very insightful about the confusions of male parenting, it does not use motherhood enough as a yardstick for measuring whether the feelings experienced by fathers are unique to them. He reasons that women continue to become pregnant and are increasingly likely to breast feed, so their roles retain some continuity. (I think he is wrong on the feeding front as bottle feeding rates are higher than they were 40 years ago, but that is not important for my analysis). Yet this assumption does not fit very easily with the figures about changes in women's lives. Roughly half of mothers now have to juggle their family and employment responsibilities – a common phenomenon in some geographical areas since industrialisation, but certainly a change in most post-war families. Recent analyses of motherhood suggest that women too find their experiences as challenging and confusing as men do theirs.

It is in the light of reports by parents of confusions in their lives that we can cast a critical eye on the survey data of both Julie Smith and Margaret O'Brien and Deborah Jones. Surveys can only give one-dimensional responses to multidimensional issues. Of course both chapters only had the space to recount a few of the findings from each study. Nevertheless I am slightly concerned that Julie Smith's analysis is too quick to assume that a change in paternal roles has taken place. My main concern is her use of very retrospective parental accounts.

The data presented by Margaret O'Brien and Deborah Jones are also open to the challenge of merely touching the surface of understanding. Yet they demonstrate their awareness of this possibility and their results are of interest. For a start, I wonder how the young people in their study formed such uniform opinions about men's attendance at childbirth or about Paternity Leave? That they had any opinions at all is perhaps a testament to the fact that fathers are much more in the public eye than continuing popular stereotypes suggest.

It is the responses on fathers as confidantes that reveal the importance of work investigating the "consumers" points of view. These teenagers appear to depict a mixed bag of relationships with their fathers, but a general distance of the father in many families. Further research is needed to clarify the nature of, and correlate with, children's views of fatherhood. At the moment we may only have tapped their more general feelings or even stereotypes.

Attempts to change men

The second theme in these papers follows from the first. If there is a problem with fathers (as suggested in the chapters reviewed above), then it will be assumed that there is a need to [re-]incorporate men into the hub of domestic activity. As Peter Moss describes, moves to enhance paternal roles have been made at a European level. Søren Carlsen provides some interesting data from the Nordic countries to show how effective such policies have been at the national level. Both contributions are highly sensitive to the need to consider resistance to change as well as the data which appear to show greater male involvement at home, yet it is always possible that the issues are even more complex than they suggest.

Peter Moss points out that it is impossible simply to write a "shopping list" of policies to be effected in order to change the roles of men. He is keen to underline that change cannot simply be directed from on high and across the board. It is his notion of "golden opportunities" about which I am slightly concerned. This is the idea that there are turning points in the life course that social policy workers should home in on in order to implement change.

The two examples he cites are the transitions to parenthood and grandparenthood. Yet, the evidence is not clear about whether these or other moments in life really are opportunities, however much researchers might see them as such. Over the past twenty years, Peter Moss's own research on the transition to parenthood has shown the centrifugal effect on men at this time of life – fathers with young children are more likely to increase their work outside the home than at any other time in life. Unless my reading of the Scandinavian data is wrong or outdated, very few men take full opportunity of the leave that is available to them. Couples appear to play the system, by arranging each parent's leave to fit in with maternal breast feeding and rights concerning their individual incomes.

Likewise, grandfatherhood is often reported as a time when men realise their missed opportunities as carers, at both practical and psychological levels. But, there is little evidence that they suddenly change their behaviour at this point. Research on couples in retirement, when many report that they hope to seize the chance to increase the man's "input", suggests that few men realise that opportunity (Vinick & Ekerdt, 1992). So, my concerns lie in whether we as researchers with a desire for change might not see too much potential in these transitions for shifts in male domesticity.

I was not surprised that Søren Carlsen found that in Denmark men who do take up Parental Leave tend to be public service employees, to work with women and to be better educated. But does this really suggest that there is an "A team" of permanently employed and well educated workers, more often in public sector jobs, who are more committed to gender equality, and a "B team" of other workers who are resistant to change? My concerns are twofold. In the first place, I worry about how selection for the "A team" actually takes place. We know of a number of correlated factors but we do not fully grasp how they fit together. For example, it might be the case that public service employees are simply more aware of their rights or have more trade union support for their desire to take leave.

There might be a number of reasons for men taking leave which are unrelated to the opportunities offered to provide and share child care. For example, there are anecdotal reports that men might take up leave to engage in activities which are not connected with parentcraft, like completing the extension to the garage while grandma looks after the new baby. Thus, secondly and more importantly, we have not yet fully grasped the effects of provision for families, like government Parental Leave schemes. We need to know, for example, about how parenting is affected by such leave policies.

We also need to know whether there are marked effects of taking such leave. I would be highly suspicious of any data showing long term "effects" on the child's IQ or on maternal well-being, as again cause–effect relationships would be almost impossible to tease apart. At the root of all these meanderings I am concerned that the "A team" might not be as valiant as they seem – the change they appear to demonstrate may be illusory.

So, does my analysis of the chapters in this book get us anywhere? Before I answer this question, let me reiterate the point that my response to the chapters in this book has been made as a devil's advocate, rather than in direct criticism of the individual authors. Yet I hope to have made the point that an analysis of fathers' contributions to family life should take into account all the perspectives reflected in the chapters in this book – in terms of historical images and tradition (Julie Smith), conflicting expectations of men (Sean French and Angela Phillips), socialisation patterns (Margaret O'Brien and Deborah Jones), work–family relations (cf the data in Søren Carlsen's chapter) and social practices and policies (Peter Moss). Each of these perspectives on its own is informative, but only together will they depict the status of contemporary fatherhood and allow us to discern what opportunities might be open to fathers.

References

Cobbett W. (1828–32) *Advice to Young Men*, Oxford: Oxford University Press (1980: George Sprater [ed.])

Eiduson, B. et al. (1982) "Comparison of socialisation practices in traditional and alternative families', in M. Lamb (ed.) *Nontraditional Families*, Hillsdale, NJ: Erlbaum

Kruk, E. (1993) *Divorce and Disengagement*, Halifax, Nova Scotia: Fernwood

La Rossa, R et al. (1991) "The fluctuating image of the 20th century American father", *Journal of Marriage and the Family*, 53, 987-977

Lamb, M. E. and Oppenheim, D. (1989) "Father and Father–Child Relationships: 5 years of research" (pp 11–26), in F. G. Cath *Fathers and their Families*, Hillsdale: Analytic Press

Lewis, C. (1986) *Becoming a Father*, Milton Keynes: Open University Press

Oakley, A (1979) *Becoming a Mother*, Oxford: Martin Robertson

Vinick, B. H. and Ekerdt, D. J. (1992) "Couples view retirement activities: expectation versus experience", in M. Szinovacz., D. Ekerdt. and B. Vinick (eds.) *Families and Retirement*, London: Sage

INDEX

HMSO

HMSO publications are available from:

HMSO Publications Centre
(Mail, fax and telephone orders only)
PO Box 276, London, SW8 5DT
Telephone orders 071-873 9090
General enquiries 071-873 0011
(queuing system in operation for both numbers)
Fax orders 071-873 8200

HMSO Bookshops
71 Lothian Road, Edinburgh, EH3 9AZ
0131-228 4181 Fax 0131-229 2734
49 High Holborn, London, WC1V 6HB
0171-873 0011 Fax 0171-873 8200 (counter service only)
68-69 Bell Street, Birmingham, B4 6AD
0121-236 9696 Fax 0121-236 9699
33 Wine Street, Bristol, BS1 2BQ
0121-236 9696 Fax 0121-236 9696
9-21 Princess Street, Manchester, M60 8AS
0161-834 7201 Fax 0161-833 0634
16 Arthur Street, Belfast, BT1 4GD
01232 238451 Fax 01232 235401
The HMSO Oriel Bookshop, The Friary,
Cardiff CF1 4AA
01222 395548 Fax 01222 384347

HMSO's Accredited Agents
(see Yellow Pages)

and through good booksellers

Printed in Scotland for HMSO Scotland by CC No37907 70C 12/95

FATHER FIGURES